Praise for *Free Book*

"Brian Tome carefully differentiates between freedom and libertinism. He makes clear that freedom requires breaking those chains, whether they are religious or secular, that keep us from actualizing what God wants for us to be."

Tony Campolo
Author of *Red Letter Christians*
Eastern University

"Brian Tome is passionate about freedom—a passion that shines through each page of this book. I am grateful to have a friend like him on the great adventure God calls us to, an adventure that can only be experienced in God's freedom."

Gary Haugen
President, International Justice Mission

"I want to stick *Free Book* in the hands of my 22-year-old neighbor searching for freedom and flirting with faith. Great book! Awesome idea, well-written, and a very needed study that I'll recommend to nonbelievers and crusty religious types alike! I loved reading the Brian-in-your-face writing style—I felt like I was sitting across the table from him."

John Burke
Author of *Soul Revolution* and *No Perfect People Allowed*

"The *Free Book* is a remarkably insightful, boldly anti-religious, immensely practical, brutally honest, incredibly entertaining and profound liberating masterpiece! Everyone who associates God with 'being religious' or 'following rules' —or anything other than joyous, life-giving freedom—needs to read this book."

Greg Boyd, Ph.D.
Author of *The Myth of a Christian Religion*
Senior Pastor, Woodland Hills Church, St. Paul, MN

"Brian Tome's new book, *Free Book*, gives 'in your face' insight to what it means to walk in God's freedom. You'll walk away feeling inspired to dream, take risks, and live the life of fullness Christ died to give us."

Craig Groeschel
Author of *It—How Church Leaders Can Find It and Keep It*
Pastor of LifeChurch.tv

"The world has never had a good definition of the word liberty, and the American people, just now, are in want of one."

Abraham Lincoln

Free Book*

I am a fanatic about freedom. And I'm fanatical about coming at you hard in this book. I'm tired of seeing people beaten down by the world's systems and by religion. I'm sick of seeing people live safe, predictable lives while their God-given passions die. God's offering real freedom. Get yours.

Brian Tome

THOMAS NELSON®
Since 1798

NASHVILLE   DALLAS   MEXICO CITY   RIO DE JANEIRO

* We haven't stayed in business for over 200 years by giving away free books.

Published in Nashville, Tennessee, by Thomas Nelson. Thomas Nelson is a registered trademark of Thomas Nelson, Inc.

Thomas Nelson, Inc., titles may be purchased in bulk for educational, business, fund-raising, or sales promotional use. For information, please e-mail SpecialMarkets@thomasnelson.com.

All Scripture quotations, unless otherwise indicated, are taken from the HOLY BIBLE, NEW INTERNATIONAL VERSION®. © 1973, 1978, 1984 by International Bible Society. Used by permission of Zondervan. All rights reserved.

Other Scripture references are from the following sources:

THE ENGLISH STANDARD VERSION. © 2001 by Crossway Bibles, a division of Good News Publishers.

The Message (MSG) by Eugene H. Peterson. © 1993, 1994, 1995, 1996, 2000. Used by permission of NavPress Publishing Group. All rights reserved.

Holy Bible, Today's New International Version®. TNIV®. © 2002, 2004 by International Bible Society. Used by permission of Zondervan. All rights reserved.

Library of Congress Cataloging-in-Publication Data

Tome, Brian.
 Free book : I am a fanatic about freedom and I'm fanatical about coming at you hard in this book, I'm tired of seeing people beaten down by the world's systems and by religion, I'm sick of seeing people live safe, predictable lives while their God-given passion dies, God's offering real freedom, get yours / Brian Tome.
  p. cm.
 ISBN 978-0-8499-2006-6 (pbk.)
 1. Liberty—Religious aspects—Christianity. 2. Fear—Religious aspects—Christianity. 3. Spirituality. 4. Christian life. I. Title.
 BT810.3.T66 2009
 234'.9—dc22   2009023463

Printed in the United States of America

10 11 12 13 RRD 9 8 7 6 5 4 3 2 1

Acknowledgments

When I've read acknowledgments in other books I've never understood the trite-sounding phrase, "This has been a labor of love," until now. It isn't just because I'm fired up about freedom. It's also because of the team that made me love this labor.

Libby, Lena, Jake, and Moriah Tome: A family that cheers me on in my freedom.

Liz Young: No way this book would have happened without her. She is a great writer and great thinker who frees me from bad grammar and disjointed ideas.

Steven Manuel: A friend and giant in the faith whose insights and fingerprints are all over this book.

Matt Chandler: For stepping in at the bottom of the ninth.

Darin Yates: A leader who quietly makes Crossroads' infrastructure healthy, and in the process, frees me for things like writing books and riding bikes.

Crossroads: A church that frees me to be fully me.

Thomas Nelson: Matt Baugher, Jennifer McNeil, and the rest of the team have been a pleasure to work with in taking a risk on me and my ideas. Maybe this time you'll make some money.

Contents

Chapter 1

The End of Fear

I am a fanatic about freedom.

When actor Charlie Sheen was using drugs, his dad, Martin Sheen, says he became a fanatic: "When a life is at stake and it's your child's, you become fearless in a lot of ways. I mean, you just become a fanatic. Nothing ever gets done unless it's done by a fanatic."[1]

I'm fanatical about coming at you hard in this book. I'm tired of seeing people beaten down by the world's systems and by religion. I'm sick of seeing people live safe, predictable lives while their God-given passions die. I hate the assumption that getting close to God means more rules and restrictions. I'm also pissed that I'll have to fight to keep the word *pissed* in this book because the publisher will want to cave to more conservative types who want to keep everyone boxed into a specific type of language.

Let's get over ourselves. Let's get over such fearful living.

Right now, I'm living in freedom and loving it. It's the most helpful grid through which I make decisions, and it's my biggest joy. Nothing else works for me—no set of rules, no self-improvement plan, no religion. My life isn't perfect, and I've had to work through some hard spots, but now I'm experiencing

1. Nancy Perry Graham, "Martin Sheen: Breaking Through," AARP, (July and August 2008) http://www.aarpmagazine.org/entertainment/martin_sheen_breaking_through.html.

the kind of freedom God offers—and it's a blast. That's why I'm writing this: I want you to experience the same thing.

As I live out freedom, though, the things I say might cause objections. Bible thumpers could be concerned that I'm not honoring God. Psychologists could be concerned that I'm a narcissistic daredevil. Most Americans will be concerned that I'm being irresponsible. But like I said, I'm a fanatic about freedom, so I'm giving this all I've got.

Tackling freedom is like joining a revolution—and that revolution is happening in the communities I encounter. Jesus' message floored His culture, just like it floors ours. His main thing was teaching about the Kingdom of God, and the freedom that kingdom offers is a revolution that gets people fired up because they're experiencing God's love and giving it to others. This kingdom was and is completely unexpected. While people expected the Messiah to bring a huge street rebellion or a rigid institution of new religious laws, instead they got Jesus saying, "Love each other, love Me, and you will experience the best of this life."

We don't need another book about the cross. As offensive as that statement might sound, it's true. That important topic has been dissected every which way possible. But a book on freedom? Yes. We need it badly. Nearly all of the "Christian literature" you'll find about freedom is telling us to *limit* our freedom. Really?! What about "Where the Spirit of the Lord is, there is freedom"?[2] The Bible doesn't say, "Where the Spirit of the Lord is, there is *restriction*," or "Where the Spirit of the

2. 2 Corinthians 3:17.

Lord is, there is *morality*." And the Bible definitely doesn't say, "Where the Spirit of the Lord is, there is *fear*."

We sing that America is "the land of the free and the home of the brave." It may be true that our Constitution protects our liberties like no other country, but if you look at the way we really function, it's according to fear. A better descriptor of us today is that we're the Land of the Fear and the Home of the Slave. Fear obstructs our understanding and route to freedom. In fact, it is the single biggest enemy of freedom, and it isn't until you get to the other side of fear that you experience the good stuff.

Have you noticed how nearly all lead news stories are based on fear? "Your microwave could kill you! Shocking details at eleven." Media is more enthusiastic about reporting on the economy's downturn than its upturn, reporting rape cases more often than rescues, and broadcasting people's mistakes rather than their successes. Even though we're watching and reading to be informed, in reality most media organizations exist only to hold our attention long enough for us to watch the advertising—where they make the big green. Unfortunately for us, we're drawn to things that strike fear and paranoia into us or things that make us believe that if we have this new "information," the things we fear won't happen.

We lead the world in popping pills to make us feel better, and we go through endless therapy for things we can't get freed from. We brace ourselves when something bad happens because "tragedy comes in threes." We can't fully enjoy a trip to the beach because we're afraid of getting skin cancer. We avoid the "bad" parts of the city and subconsciously teach our children to fear anyone who isn't from our own culture. We're so nervous about the reputation of Halloween and poisoned candy that we can't sit outside with our neighbors and eat KitKats together. We won't spend time with homosexuals because we're heterosexual and we fear that maybe we'll send them the wrong message, so we miss out on a person's individuality and on becoming engaged in his or her life.

American Christians, especially, live in this Land of Fear. That's ironic, because the core of the Christ-following life is about overcoming fear and bondage. The entire Kingdom of God is about freedom. "It is for freedom that Christ set us free."[3] We've been freed from sin, and therefore we are free to have joy. Why is that so hard for us to accept? The Bible says God hasn't given us a spirit of fear, but a spirit of power, love, and self-discipline.[4] This means that whenever we feel fearful, we are out of sync with the Spirit of God for that moment.

Here's something else to think about: fear is the starting point of purchasing insurance. There isn't another society in the world's history that has had as much insurance as modern-day Americans do. I'm calling myself out here, because I have every kind of insurance known to man: life, disability, medical, auto, home, canine. (Okay, I don't have canine insurance, but I'm sure I have some type of coverage to protect me in the event of Stanley's untimely demise.) Now, given my stage in life and my financial standing and obligations, I think it's responsible for me to have this coverage, but I can't help wondering if an unrealistic fear of the unknown causes me to pass

3. Galatians 5:1.
4. 2 Timothy 1:7.

this off as "responsible" when it might just be really neurotic. Is insurance bad? No. But what's bad is that some of us are trying to purchase security. Insurance can't give us security or power; only God can.

When I was a kid, I broke bones three times when riding my bike. Yet I kept riding. Without a helmet too—as God intended. How many of us had helmets when we were growing up? If you are over forty years old, you know where I'm going with this. *No one* wore a helmet while riding a bicycle. If my friends had caught me wearing a helmet, they would have beaten me about the head with blunt objects. We didn't go river rafting with helmets. We didn't do ropes courses with helmets. Yet, if I'd invested in helmet stock when I was eighteen, I'd be a millionaire right now.

I'm not really against helmets. What I'm against is their representation of our fear. (I don't mean to offend you, but if you put a helmet on your three-year-old when he's in the basement riding his tricycle, you are overly fearful, and you're probably conditioning your child to be fearful.)

Remember the controversy around the Beijing Olympics when China's female gymnasts were called out for being too young to compete? The MSNBC article "Why Restrict Ages Anyway?" said this: "The reason the Chinese might have to tell a fib? Simple, young girls make perfect gymnasts, with their bodies and minds uncluttered with the fear of falling and failure."[5]

I don't want to live a life cluttered with the fear of falling

5. Associated Press, "Why Restrict Ages Anyway?" NBC Olympics Web site, http://www
.nbcolympics.com/gymnastics/news/newsid=249420.html.

and failure. One statement I make to myself—and this represents my opposition to fear—is that when riding my motorcycle in states that don't require helmets, I don't wear one. I hesitate to write this because I anticipate that many of you will immediately lose respect for me and give me guilt. You'll think I'm reckless, selfish, or stupid. Okay, maybe I am stupid. No doubt that if I wreck and suffer brain damage that a helmet would have saved me from, I'll regret riding with only my bandanna. But on all those days that I don't wreck, I win. I don't have wind fighting my helmet, and I don't get those endless vibrations that slightly blur my vision. My head is cooler, and, of course, I look cooler.

There's a tension, of course, between acting responsibly and acting out of fear. I recognize that. But God regularly embraces people who do dangerous things. A guy named David kills a lion. Samson takes a donkey's jawbone and uses it as a hatchet to kill his enemies. Esther risks death and confronts a king. Paul continually gets in situations where he's shipwrecked, beaten, and abused. If we think something isn't "safe," we think God's not into it. It's time to change that mentality, because God was in all of the above and in much of what we may be denying ourselves or running away from. Fear might keep you from going places you could enjoy, talking with people who could expand your thinking, and trying things that will grow you.

I also believe that fear is not just a negative emotion—it's a cancer. It's a full-on assault from an evil force who wants you belittled and your life (your living-life-for-all-it's-worth-and-going-for-the-gusto life) destroyed. If we saw someone in a casket at the end of his life, surrounded by people saying, "He was responsible, rational, and upstanding," then we should conclude, *No, fear sapped the vigor out of who this guy really could have been*. I don't want that for you. I want you to experience what Jesus meant when He said, "I have come that they may have life, and have it to the *full*."[6]

God's primary mission is liberation. He not only wants to liberate us from our fears, grievances, addictions, petty pre-occupations, and dozens of other distractions—but He's also about freeing the very planet we live on: "That the creation itself will be liberated from its bondage to decay and brought into the freedom and glory of the children of God."[7]

By the way, I'm going to use a lot of Scripture in this book. I'm not assuming you believe everything in the Bible, but you'll see that these freedom thoughts aren't mine but ancient, deep-stream wisdom. If you do believe the Bible, you'll see that you can't get away from the freedom message.

This book is about you having a life void of fear and rife with freedom. It's about casting off whatever hinders you and going after the grand adventure of experiencing God while you experience all of life. You can have peace—living free from the burdens of your past mistakes and others' expecta-tions. You can wake up excited and full of hope. You can have the sort of joy you thought only kids could have. And best I can, I want to help you get there.

If you are up for this message, strap on your helmet and let's get started. Or better yet, take it off.

6. John 10:10, emphasis mine.
7. Romans 8:21 TNIV.

Chapter 2 ————————————————

The Death of Religion

A guy was drinking a Bloody Mary in our church parking lot the other morning. We were tailgating—it was Super Bowl weekend—and the day was close to perfect. Football, trucks, fire pits, hot dogs, and beer? Perfect.

But not everyone thought it was perfect. If you haven't heard, church parking lots aren't supposed to host tailgates, and Bloody Marys are off-limits when you're fifty yards from a church door. So, apparently, we needed some reprimanding. It came in an e-mail:

>> I'm deeply offended and greatly disappointed by Crossroads' involvement with alcohol during the Super Bowl event. Such a move can be personally and spiritually devastating for people like myself [with an alcoholic past]. Will your next event involve weed or porn?!

Now honestly, I thought about calling this guy and saying, "Great idea! We love weed around here!" until I realized he probably wasn't in the mood for my sarcasm. Instead, I e-mailed back:

>> No, we won't be having weed or porn. We believe those things are wrong under every circumstance. But we don't

believe alcohol is wrong under every circumstance. And I could quote you many scriptures about this, but then you'd probably have some to quote as well.

Then I added:

>> We don't want to cause anyone to stumble, and I don't think we caused you to stumble, either. Unless we consider giving you an opportunity to judge us as "stumbling." [That wasn't sarcasm, I promise.]

Here's the thing: thousands upon thousands of people have come to Crossroads, found Jesus, found forgiveness, found purpose, been baptized, and received grace. These are people with different beliefs, different cultures, and different piercings. And thousands of those people have gone back to their friends and shared what they found inside: authentic freedom. It's that simple.

Now, alcohol isn't an agent of freedom. In fact, it isn't even right for everyone to drink. (Some need to avoid it entirely because of how it makes them act or what's in their past.) What I'm saying is that it seems as though many of us are so fearful of only doing what's "right" that we've lost sight of the life Jesus came to give us. He came not to give us a life of abstinence but of abundance. Abundant alcohol? No. Abundant freedom.

How would you naturally complete the following sentence: "God's main thing is that He wants me to be _____"? What goes in your blank?

For most of my life I would have said something like, "God

wants me to be moral." Or "God wants me to be spiritual." Or "God wants me to be good." Or "God wants me to sort my recyclables." But according to the Bible, the answer is "free." This is a pretty big shift from what most religions tell you, and it's the shift I had to make to understand freedom.

Somewhere along the way, the message and reputation of the Bible (and therefore man's idea of God) got reversed. Instead of people recognizing it was a message about total freedom and perfect love, the Bible unjustly earned a reputation for being a book of restrictions. But that's because of who has been representing it.

I don't think this is big news: many Christians are oppressive. When they're paraded on TV, all you see are the bad haircuts, and all you hear are the "should nots"—and the entire portrayal is guilt-ridden and sensationalized. And when it's not about the "should nots," it's about the "shoulds": "you should tithe; you should read the Bible; you should serve the poor"—and that message can be just as filled with guilt and misconceptions. There's no grace in that, and there's only a portion of the truth. No wonder people run from the guy wearing a gold cross lapel pin. Whatever happened to "You should enjoy your life"? How about some religious jewelry with that one?

I think a lot of Christ-followers are afraid of this freedom and grace idea. They think, *What will people do if they believe they have complete freedom as a Christ-follower?* Maybe they assume lives will get chaotic and out of control. They think people will become "of the world" instead of "of God." They worry that Christians will get a bad reputation. Guess what? For the most part, Christians already do have a bad reputation.

I've been around the religious scene for a long time. When you're the son of a church organist and have been a Christian for twenty-seven years—and a professional paid Christian for twenty years and the lead pastor of a church for twelve of those twenty—you inevitably go through "Christianity movements." There's no shortage: personal salvation (being "saved" is the most important moment of one's life), second touch of the Holy Spirit (you get a turbo-charged empowerment from God), social action (it's all about what work you do), moralism (laws and obedience make us holy), total grace (Jesus came solely to give grace and offer a burden-free life), and on and on. While all these movements are important in part and have scriptures to back them up, the overall theme of the Bible and Christ-following life is freedom. In fact, it's where the Bible begins. God creates a man and woman and gives them the autonomy to make a home, name the animals, create a business plan for their agriculture, and have sex—all at their own discretion.

> God blessed them [Adam and Eve] and said to them: "Be fruitful and increase in number; fill the earth and subdue it. Rule over the fish of the sea and the birds of the air and over every living creature that moves on the ground."
>
> Then God said, "I give you every seed-bearing plant on the face of the whole earth and every tree that has fruit with seed in it. They will be yours for food. And to all the beasts of the earth and all the birds of the air and all the creatures that move on the ground—everything that has the breath of life in it—I give every green plant for food." And it was so.

God saw all that he had made, and it was very good.[1]

God didn't start things on earth with an iron fist. He started with amazing gifts, ownership, and the okay to make big decisions. He wanted people who would think for themselves, create, manage, and be fulfilled. He doesn't want a field of machinelike followers who memorize rhetoric and ask permission for every step forward. He doesn't want followers who are bogged down by anxiety. He wants imaginative, fulfilled, and dynamic followers who are running right alongside Him.

One of the most contentious things that early followers of Jesus were divided over was the "right" diet, because before Jesus, this culture had an intense history of strict laws and spare grace. So many influential Jewish believers in Jesus were convinced that Gentile (non-Jewish) believers should follow all the ancient dietary practices. Yet, Paul—one of Jesus' closest followers—saw those restrictions as limited to a specific people in a specific place and time. (And maybe he just felt sorry for the taste buds of people who never snacked on bacon-wrapped shrimp.)

Paul seemed to arrive at his conviction through the intersection of his mission, what he read in Scripture, and what he saw in the lives of those who knew Jesus. He realized that asking people to change their eating habits seemed both petty and unproductive. Imagine if you didn't know Jesus today and someone was trying to lead you to living your life with Him, but he or she made sure you understood that you could

1. Genesis 1:28–31.

never have a bratwurst again. You would wonder what kind of God you were being asked to follow—and probably decline being serious about a God with such a judgmental palate.

Through Paul, God made it clear that the spirit of the law was above the letter of the law: "Therefore do not let anyone judge you by what you eat or drink, or with regard to . . . a New Moon celebration or a Sabbath day. These are a shadow of the things that were to come; the reality, however, is found in Christ."[2] Paul said people were free to eat virtually anything they wanted. This freedom even extended to meat that was previously sacrificed in a Pagan worship service—a radical move for that culture.

Instead of exalting and celebrating that freedom, we now have untold numbers of books, articles, and commentaries devoted to making sure we don't cause someone to "stumble" if they don't feel free to experience what you're experiencing. I'm not trying to give a full exposition here. Yet I must say this: most people interpret this issue to mean that, in regard to anything questionable, we should not do *anything* that would raise someone else's eyebrows. But in my Bible, these scriptures come from a section called "The Believer's Freedom"!

Instead of being so concerned about what might happen if you get too close to the proverbial line—because there are plenty of those messages out there—we need more voices saying, "You are free, and don't allow anyone to bum you out by judging you." That message is in the Bible. It needs to be in you too.

What does living by the "letter of the law" versus the "spirit of the law" look like in religion today? Believing that you have

2. Colossians 2:16–17.

to find the exact "calling" God has for you before you can do anything worthwhile, that you have to date exactly the right person all the time, or that you have to make up for your sins by doing community service. Those are the kinds of laws that will pull you under and eventually cause burnout. Here's the truth: "The only thing that counts is faith expressing itself through love."[3]

Freedom is being who God designed you to be. It's living free of condemnation and free of others' concern. It's developing a healthy conscience and not allowing things in your past that you've repented and been forgiven of to still taint your conscience. It's believing that if God is okay with you, then who gives a rip if someone else isn't? Freedom is about seeing possibilities and knowing that God is okay with us going after those possibilities—instead of fixating on whether there is a different way that He might like more.

God is not a bad Santa trying to find everything that's wrong with you. He wants the best for you. He wants you to go into meetings and not worry about what other people will think of you because you're free to be who you really are. Those times when you have too much month at the end of your money? He wants you to realize that shortage doesn't dictate who you are or determine your self-worth or how you appear to other people. When you get all religious and start thinking you have to earn God's favor—that you can do better, be better, be worthy—God wants you to just relax and realize you're fully loved no matter what you do or what you've done.

3. Galatians 5:6.

What would it be like if, no matter where you went or what happened the night before or how you screwed up and hurt someone, you knew and believed you had God's favor? What would it be like if you had the kinds of interactions with other people that really mattered and weren't just superficial connections? And what if no matter what you had done—no matter how much porn you had looked at, how verbally abusive you had been, how many times you had manipulated and lied—you knew God was still hanging around and loving you?

God has already removed the biggest burdens from your life, and now you get to be who you were designed to be, regardless of what anybody else has to say about it.

I've seen and experienced people who have been freed because they accepted the literal message of Jesus: artists who stopped self-obsessing and began living amazing lives; recovering alcoholics who stopped calling themselves alcoholics because they were finished being defined that way; husbands who asked their wives for forgiveness and began restoring marriages; mothers who received the fullness of grace and began letting their guard down.

In the Bible's book of Psalms, David, a shepherd who became the king of Israel, wrote, "I will walk about in freedom, for I have sought out your [God's] precepts."[4] In other words, when any of us seeks God's ways, we will find exactly what we need: freedom. There's no other way.

The day of freedom is here.

4. Psalm 119:45.

Chapter 3

The Freedom Giver

A group of my friends are in Mumbai, India, right now. We've been working to rescue young girls from forced prostitution and move them into aftercare homes where they're protected and loved into a new way of life. The brothel and pimp situation, especially for these young girls, is as horrific as you could imagine. I could write at length about it (and also about the astonishing hope coming out of many situations), but here's the fascinating part about how these girls respond to their freedom: they resist it.

When the brothel doors are broken through and security arrives, the girls fight against their liberators and cry fearful tears as they are being ushered to freedom. They don't understand what is being offered. They've become so accustomed to their slavery and abuse—often mistaking it for love and security—that they can't imagine an alternative. Sometimes, even when they're rescued and given safe beds, food, guidance, and protection, they run away. They would rather have the known—a horrible and dehumanizing situation—than the unknown of freedom.

Freedom isn't always obvious. It might be entirely different from what you're accustomed to. It can be unexpected and countercultural—a far cry from the world's systems.

Sometimes we think we have a pretty good idea of what

freedom is like. Maybe we lie our way through business deals because they're lucrative and we want the "freedom" to buy second homes. We cheat on husbands because other men seem more interested in our attention. We overstock the refrigerator because someone used to control our eating and now we want to eat anything we feel like. We dwell in the unfairness of our past and can't resist the self-pitying security of reliving it. We don't make bold decisions because we're too nervous about a misstep in our "purpose-driven" lives. We avoid close relationships as a protection device.

On the surface, a lot of these things can seem like freedom. Maybe we get an adrenaline rush or a huge check or a year of life that feels totally self-gratifying. Later, though, we realize we brought confusion upon ourselves; we dug back into pain or we sought a shallow, destructive form of freedom. The kind of freedom we were seeking had to do merely with the moment and ourselves: no authority, no boundary lines, and no one to lean on who could continually hold us up, build into us, and protect us.

If you liked the earlier part about no helmets, you're probably *not* going to like this: true freedom starts with God and His ways. Generally, when we hear the word *freedom*, we imagine a life with no boundaries in which only "yours truly" calls the shots. In America it seems we're all about getting out from under authority—not caving into it—because any sort of authority seems to be what stands in the way of our freedom. But living without any boundaries is like trying to play tennis without the lines. The game would be a mess.

It's not popular to talk about submission to anything or

anyone, because we imagine we want complete independence as soon as we hit junior high. Submission sounds like weakness. It conjures up images of clueless, glazed-eye followers or the yes-man coworker. Of course, sometimes submission *is* weakness and a poor choice; sometimes we follow the wrong leader or the wrong manifestos and get screwed up in the process. But sometimes we are merely refusing to submit and follow someone or something because we don't want to get burned again, look weak, or put aside our deeply rooted pride, so we go back to hobbling along on our crutches of fear while distrust and independence completely cage us in.

If you're rolling your eyes right now and thinking I'm nuts, consider this: how much relief would you experience if you could completely give up trying to control your relationships, your future, your every minute—and instead of controlling those things, you were able to trust someone else to manage those things for you? Imagine you're a kid again who doesn't stress out about getting the mac 'n' cheese on the table or being qualified for the perfect job. Imagine relaxing and trusting that you are completely taken care of and deeply loved.

Although it sounds counterintuitive, freedom requires a decision to follow someone, because freedom is not about your isolation and independence. It's about the one who's leading you and the way you choose to follow. You don't have to muddle through things on your own or live a fear-based life guided by trial and error. You have a God with an overarching plan—a God you don't need to impress, hang your head in front of, help out, manipulate, or plead attention from. He's a profound God who has the power to strike every one of us down but instead gives us His pure love. And that's the kind of God I want to submit to.

*

Whether we realize it or not, every one of us is a slave to something, and most of us are slaves to many things. If every career decision you make is solely economic, you might be a slave to money. If every time Apple releases a shiny new product you sleep outside the store to be first in line, you might be a slave to technology. If you find that you go into meeting after meeting wanting to impress people with your intelligence (even if it doesn't add value to the conversation), you might be a slave to your reputation. If you believe your home country never does anything wrong and its foreign policy is always right, you might be a slave to nationalism. If you always vote straight party lines and can't see any good within the opposing group, you might be a slave to politics. If you read a book by a guy who pastors a big church and assume he has some ulterior motive, such as convincing you to donate money to his cause, you might be a slave to prejudice.

I could go on and on and on. We're slaves to what we don't even realize anymore. We get in habits of bondage and have no clue we are held back. We might not even fight for release.

I know it is difficult for some people to hear the "slave and bondage" terminology. Some of you have backgrounds I don't personally have experience with, and the imagery of slavery is volatile. But if you find that anytime a white guy talks about slavery you think he has a guilty white-man's complex, you might be a slave to racism.

Many of the things I'm enslaved to will come out as I write this book, because part of experiencing freedom is being authentic, and part of sharing freedom is telling people where you get hung up. Here's an easy one: I realized recently, as I was interacting with a guy who is a national leader and a huge contributor in my city, that during our times together I would say something just to try to impress him. I'd drop some little comment or try to say something clever just to glorify myself. What I said didn't benefit the conversation. It didn't benefit anyone. It was a move to keep myself "safe" with a smart-guy image. But safe doesn't always mean free.

Most of us want this safe thing—safe life, safe image, safe house, safe travels—so we construct barriers. We stay close to our own neighborhoods and warn against others; we resist having hard conversations with our spouses; we fear sickness so much we can't get on an airplane; we worry about our image and refuse to wear the same outfit from party to party; we become the Christian who "safely" hides her mistakes so that non-Christians will think she's perfect. Do you know what happens with all this "safety"? We end up creating prisons for ourselves. We crush the enjoyment in things. We become restricted, and we restrict others. When we're slaves to materialism, we're not free to be generous. When we're slaves to lust, we're not free to love.

The same guy who told the Gentiles they could eat freely, Paul, was also the one who started a church in Rome. And Paul records the instructions he gave to those people: "Don't you know that when you offer yourselves to someone to obey him as slaves, you are slaves to the one whom you obey—whether you are slaves to sin, which leads to death, or to obedience, which leads to righteousness?"[1] Paul is saying that everybody has an overriding objective; everybody has something they submit to. We choose to follow safety, pride, independence, and selfishness—or we choose to follow generosity, authenticity, community, and freedom. In other words, you have to choose what and who you are going to be slave to, because no matter what, it will happen.

Maybe you've heard a motivational speaker or pastor share the story about Abe Lincoln at a slave-buying auction. When a young woman was put up on the auction block, Lincoln stepped forward and paid for her. As they were walking away together, Lincoln told her she was allowed to go; she didn't have to follow him. The girl, who must have been in disbelief and waiting for the catch, looked up at him and asked if he was he serious. Could she really just leave his side, go her own way, and be free?

"Yes," Lincoln answered.

"Then I choose to follow you," the girl said, keeping his stride. "Because any man who offers me freedom is the man I want to follow."

Whether or not that story is true, the important thing is that something in our spirit craves that story. We want to believe in ultimate rescue. We want to believe that someone

1. Romans 6:16.

out of nowhere is going to drop everything and start running to us. We want to experience the overwhelming shock of love. And if we did, we would willingly pledge our allegiance.

That story represents perfectly what Jesus offers when He says, "[The Spirit of the Lord] has sent me to proclaim freedom for the prisoners."[2] More than just a promise, He tells us why and how we can be free, and that our freedom is now—it is for today, not something we'll find only once we pass on to the next life. It's not just about "getting saved" so you have a bus ticket to heaven. Freedom is for *today*.

All of us need an emancipator—someone to buy us out of our old life and give us the way and means to step into something new. That emancipator is a person from the outside: never a slave owner or fellow slave. It feels like a conundrum—like it can't be true but it is. We need to willingly put ourselves under Jesus. We need to quit trying to do this on our own. First Peter 2:16 says, "Live as free people, but do not use your freedom as a cover-up for evil; live as God's slaves."

*

Our freedom does have a cost—although it's an unexpected one.

The reason the old plantation owners weren't going to just give away their slaves was that it would cost them a lot of money. It would fundamentally disrupt the foundation of the economy: a cost to the entire country, not just the bank

2. Luke 4:18.

accounts of a few men. If you think it wasn't until the Civil War that the leaders of our country started wrestling with the issue of slavery, think again. The words of our country's founders make it very clear that they understood the hypocrisy in creating a "free nation" that allowed enslaved labor. The problem was taking the hard step of change.

Joseph Ellis, in his book *Founding Brothers: The Revolutionary Generation*, puts it well when he says,

> Slavery would become the central and defining problem for the next seventy years of American history: that the inability to take decisive action against slavery in the decades immediately following the Revolution permitted the size of the enslaved population to grow exponentially. . . .[3]

Though he personally owned slaves, George Washington favored an eventual, gradual release of slaves. Some in Congress, such as Elbridge Gerry of Massachusetts, proposed allocating ten million dollars from the federal budget to compensate slave owners if they immediately set their slaves free. Others wanted to buy an island and deport all U.S. slaves there.

Although many people had a heart for the slaves' freedom, they didn't have a stomach for the cost. But for us to have our freedom, it costs something. In the overarching, eternal sense, the cost is picked up by God—not by us. We get to live with abundance because He already paid it. This

3. Joseph Ellis, *Founding Brothers: The Revolutionary Generation* (New York: Alfred A. Knopf, 2001), 88.

was and is the ultimate loving act of grace. Yet in the daily practical sense, with that cost removed, our responsibility is making the day-to-day decisions that help us keep hold of that freedom.

You and I understand justice—it's hardwired into us. The reason we don't like it when someone gets off scot-free is that God doesn't like when we get off scot-free for our pride, our lust, our addictions, our mistakes. So as that debt accumulates (whether we're realizing it or not), God has to do something about it: He has to be just. Yet His justice is surprising. God decided that Jesus—His Son—is the payment for what we owe. Jesus gathers our debt, becomes the emancipator by paying the cost, and walks *with* us along the road to freedom.

Maybe you've seen statues of a man on a cross or heard someone say, "Jesus died for your sins." But if it's never floored you, then my guess is you've never really let it sink in. You haven't come to terms with how desperately you need to be rescued. Like the sex slaves we've met in India who run back to the brothels, you haven't fully received and rested in the freedom being offered.

People who tell you that you are your own worst enemy or your own best answer are only going to help to a certain point. When you are pulling yourself up by your bootstraps, there's only so far, so high, you can go before you start walking around like a rigid idiot. Jesus tells us exactly what He's about and why we need to stop thinking we can do this life on our own. In His first public worship setting after He'd been exhaustively tested for forty days in the desert by Satan, He chose to read from the prophet Isaiah, "The Spirit of the Lord is on me, because he has anointed me to preach good news to the poor. He has sent me to proclaim freedom for the prisoners and recovery of sight for the blind, to release the oppressed, proclaim the year of the Lord's favor."[4] Jesus was saying, "God really likes you, and that's why I'm here." Then He rolled up the scroll, handed it to an attendant standing near Him, and sat down. As people continued to look at Him, He said, "Today this scripture is fulfilled in your hearing." In other words, "I'm the guy who was written about and came to bring freedom." He spelled it out. No second-guessing on who He was or what He came to do.

Jesus is the ultimate Freedom Giver.

4. Luke 4:18–19.

Chapter 4

New Identity

Libby and I took our kids on a spring break trip not too long ago. Things had been a little tight for us financially, and even as we tried to pull together money for the trip, we knew it was going to be a luxury we'd definitely appreciate.

The trip was one of those all-inclusive things, where one price gets you everything: your room, bikes, kayaks, food, beer, the works. They gave us little bracelets that marked our identities and served as our all-access passes for the vacation. (Someone asked me later if it was worth it, and here's my counsel: those all-inclusive deals are great if you're a fat alcoholic on a budget. "Just one more cheeseburger margarita combo, please.")

So after my kids drank about ten virgin strawberry daiquiris each (and proceeded to never drink one again for the remainder of the trip), we started exploring other nearby hotels. We had friends staying around the area during the same time, but we didn't know exactly where. So we figured we'd just search them out. We got on bikes, and as we pulled in the driveway at each new hotel, an employee would come out of a little shack and say something like, "Whoa, whoa, whoa. Who are you?" He was looking at our bracelets, and they didn't match the ones from his property. So we'd have this long conversation that started with, "No, we're not try- ing to mooch anything off of your property. We have plenty of cheeseburgers and margaritas where we came from." After leaving a wallet behind as collateral, we'd get into the place— when we were allowed entry, that is—but we didn't have full access to the amenities of that place unless we had the proper identification bracelet.

When you submit to and follow Jesus, you receive His ID bracelet for freedom. Full access, full benefits included.

The New Testament recounts an interaction Jesus had with a guy named Nicodemus, and it was probably like a con- versation many of us would have had with Him. Nicodemus was a highly respected guy in his community—successful in his field and in religious circles—and he had power and authority. But for some reason Nick waited until nightfall to approach Jesus (episode #1 of Nick at Nite). Maybe he was nervous, or maybe he felt that the nighttime was the right time to ask spiritual questions. He asked Jesus for some tips on how to be a follower, and Jesus responded, "Very truly I tell you, no one can see the kingdom of God without being born again."[1]

Most of us have heard that (or something like it) as a slo- gan: "Get born again." We see it on handmade signs during *Monday Night Football.* For the longest time in my journey with God, I believed that this thing Jesus said referred to how I (and everyone else) needed to get to heaven. I thought there was sort of a cosmic American Express card: "Jesus. Don't

1. John 3:3 TNIV.

leave earth without Him." But that's not what Jesus was talking about. He was talking about the Kingdom of God and how it changes life now—not just in heaven.

For Nicodemus, this "kingdom" talk would have been pretty easy to grasp. Rome was a full-on kingdom at the time, dominating the economic system, the transportation system, the pervading culture, everything. It touched every area of people's lives.

So when Jesus talked about the Kingdom of God, He was saying, "I am coming to bring about a revolution that goes against all known realities and brings them under the rule of God. I am coming to break into your world and have your whole reality be about God. I am calling *you* to this revolution." Jesus wasn't simply explaining how to get into heaven or sharing the secret password for the pearly gates. Instead, Jesus was telling Nicodemus that He gives followers a total overhaul of their lives—a fresh, new start. A new identity. He does this not because He has a king complex or wants to rule with an iron fist; He does it because He knows the world's systems are broken and lead to bondage because they're manipulated by broken humans. The only answer is God.

Nicodemus wasn't thrilled with the idea of a "rebirth." Maybe you're thinking the same thing. He asked Jesus how anyone could be born again when they're old. Surely, he said, we can't enter the womb for a second time. He wasn't dumb. He understood metaphors, so he wasn't asking literally how a full-grown man could get back inside the birth canal. He understood exactly what Jesus was saying, and he didn't like it. He was saying, "You're telling me I have to start all over? That I have to give up everything I believed up to this point—all my success, religious accomplishments, and accolades—and take on a whole new beginning? That's not what I had in mind, Jesus. I just wanted a few spiritual insights to enhance my life."

Many of us can empathize. We don't feel like total screw-ups; we just want a few helpful spiritual principles. But here's the thing: if you want God—all of God, all the freedom, the 100 percent full-octane life—you have to have a brand-new beginning. You have to fully abandon your past life. You have to be willing to die to yourself. It isn't that everything in your life needs to be changed out for something new. You're not being asked to give *up* everything you have—you're being asked to give *over*. Jesus says that being born again is not about what we do. Rather, it's about what *He* does. It's a relief, and also an adventure.

The possibility for Eternal Life doesn't start when you die. Eternal Life begins now. Just because you have been "born again," in a going-to-heaven sense, doesn't mean you have the kind of free life right now that Jesus affords. In order to get free you may need to take on the humble posture that Jesus mandated that Nicodemus go through. You may need to start all over on some of your assumptions and allow God to do something new in you.

Jesus said to Nicodemus, "Flesh gives birth to flesh, but the Spirit gives birth to spirit."[2] In other words, you have natural abilities. You might have tons of abilities, or you might have

2. John 3:6 TNIV.

made a good show of this life. But what Jesus is saying is that if you're satisfied with what your own natural abilities can get, you can have what your own efforts can get you. That's "flesh giving birth to flesh." Flesh is your natural inclination and what you can do on your own. The Spirit, though, gives birth to spirit. In other words, if we want the spiritual freedom that God offers us, only He can give us that new birth. If you're not willing to die to yourself and receive this new, God-fueled birth, you're not getting the full power He offers. Jesus is offering you His own identity; He's giving you the full-access pass. No guy at a hotel gate is going to stop and ask why you're mooching. No concierge is going to ask how you got the bracelet or what you did to earn it.

Some of us don't want to let go of our old identity even when it's a crappy one. Because of the twisted appeal of bondage—bondage to our pain, our shame, our past—we hang on tight to it. We'd prefer saying, "That's just the way I am because of _____ and _____," instead of saying, "Yeah, that's something I'm working on changing."

A musician friend of mine used to get a lot of attention for all the negative things that happened to him and even all the mistakes he made. His identity was directly linked to his pain, and through the sympathy he got from others, it was easy to dwell in that. He made the decision to change, though. Now, he gets attention by loving and encouraging others. He doesn't go around moaning about his past; instead, he focuses on the goodness of today and the future.

How do we receive a new identity? Some people will tell you it's by saying a certain prayer. Some people will say, "Just come on down the aisle and you'll get reborn." But nowhere in Scripture does anybody need a building to get reborn. Nowhere in Scripture does it say that taking on God's identity happens automatically during a water baptism (though maybe it will, for you). There's not a formula for how it has to happen.

A few months ago one of my friends decided to accept this rebirth. He was watching *The Dukes of Hazzard*. (How's that for not following a formula?) Now, this wouldn't probably have worked for me—filling my head with Daisy Duke images—but for my friend, this is when it hit. Something clicked. All of the sudden he said, "Do you know what? I believe this stuff." Suddenly he was overwhelmed by the freedom Jesus was offering, and he knew it would create an entirely different trajectory for his life. It wouldn't be a passive thing. It would be a revolution.

So what do you have to do? Receive. You don't need to work on your morality. You don't need to figure out a perfect prayer life first. You just receive. Then the fullness of God— all His grace, all His Spirit, all His power—are yours. This is where life takes off.

Here are some amazing words to rest in: "Both the one who makes men holy and those who are made holy are of the same family."[3] That's Jesus calling you a brother or a sister. You're not being called a servant or slave. When you have received Him, you're not being called a big fat sinner who doesn't deserve to be happy. You're being called pure, holy,

3. Hebrews 2:11.

loved. What does that mean to us on earth? It means you're as holy and righteous as Billy Graham, Mother Teresa, even Jesus. Yes, you are as holy as Jesus when you die to your old self and receive your new identity. You're not just going to be holy at some point in the future or just holy in heaven. You're holy now. And you can have this holiness because Jesus sacrificed Himself. He took on a mortal death because it was the only way to rescue humanity. So we are not "divine" in our natural selves; we are not divine because we are human and we deserve the best of the best. We are divine because Jesus took what we actually deserve—punishment, death—and intervened through His grace.

Getting a new identity brings freedom because you no longer have to be defined by your family, your spouse, your coworkers, your teachers, or your neighbors.

I have two parents, Dick and Eileen Tome, for whom I'm very thankful. I've been under their care since birth. Prior to birth I formed another bond with the woman who brought me into this world. I'm adopted and proud of it. But according to the conviction of Nancy Verrier, who wrote the book *Primal Wound*, there could repercussions.

As the theory goes, even though I have no formal memory of my birth mother, I formed a primal bond with her in utero. When I was handed over into the loving arms of Dick and Eileen Tome, something inside of me noticed that the only human I had ever known was gone, leaving me with a sense of abandonment. For most of my life I've categorized this sort of theorizing as psychobabble. But over the past couple years I've noticed that I feel unduly hurt when someone leaves the church I pastor. For every person who leaves we gain several new people, but nonetheless, when I hear someone has left, I feel wounded and wonder if they are a part of some sort of campaign to hurt me.

I don't know how much water is in the adoption theory, but this I know: regularly feeling hurt or abandoned happens when you aren't free. To be fully free I need to notice this faulty pattern in my mind and renew my mind in accordance with how God says it needs to operate.

With this new identity, our problems don't all fall away. We still live in a world where evil exists, where other people will harm us and we'll harm others. We'll all make mistakes again and again until we leave this earth. So there might be more terrorist attacks. More children will die. More marriages will fail. More lies will be told.

But with Jesus, you have access to power that you didn't have before. Not only do you have much to offer this world because of your new identity, but you have an amazing freedom to experience because you are no longer restricted.

You—*you*—were worth dying for.

And you are beautiful.

You are holy.

You are free.

Chapter 5 ———————

Forgiveness Freeway

t is time for some practical applications and experiments. Life experience and the Bible's message tell me that the most common means to bondage is bitterness, and the key to getting out of that cell is forgiveness. The forgiveness freeway recognizes that I must easily "on-ramp" by offering forgiveness, and I must not easily "off-ramp" to exits of bitterness, entitlement, anger, and vengeance.

Part 1: Receiving Forgiveness

Wilkinsburg, Pennsylvania, is just a few miles from my hometown. In 1986, when they were celebrating their centennial, the town went looking for a time capsule from 1962. They couldn't find it. They found the one from 1912, but not 1962. Gas City, Indiana, had the same problem in 1992, but they had a tenacious leader. The mayor encouraged residents to dig around the city hall for a fifty-year-old capsule. Thirty holes and one broken flagpole later, they gave up.

There's an official organization called the Time Capsule Society, and they report that 90 percent of buried cylinders are never recovered. What would it be like if our problems, mistakes, faults, and offenses were buried—never to be seen again? Wouldn't that be comforting? What new freedom would we experience?

We all try to do this at some point: we try to cover up or deny that we've done anything wrong. Or we put the blame on another person. Or we pretend there's a statute of limitations, and if no one has dug it up—or if nothing bad has happened for a while—then we're in the clear.

This approach might work to some extent when, legally speaking, we've done something wrong to another person, but what about when we have wronged God? God doesn't suffer from memory loss. Playing the blame game with Him doesn't work, because God knows the truth and can't be convinced otherwise. Not only that, but the way we treat other people—His children created in His image—is something He takes personally.

Have you ever had someone leave you a cold message that goes something like, "Hey Brian, could you call me? There's something we have to discuss"? If your first reaction is one of fear, dread, or a churning stomach, you may be having a physiological reaction to a spiritual reality: you are burying or denying something that must be handled. Maybe you are running through your mind all the things you've done wrong and may have been caught for. It's even likely that before you call the person back, you have the top two or three potential offenses along with a corresponding alibi organized in your mind.

This is no way to live. It takes too much energy and too many stomach enzymes. This is living in bondage. Pangs of guilt or angst are signs that we don't have full freedom. Being free includes having a life that is atoned for. One in which you don't dread bumping into someone in the store. One in which no voicemail will bum you out. One in which you have no shame talking about anything that's happened in your life.

This doesn't mean that you haven't done shameful things. Rather, it means you have dealt with your past sins and aren't worried you'll be found out. Dealing with a shameful past means confessing the incident not just to people who are "safe," but perhaps also to the person you have sinned against. The Bible says, "Therefore confess your sins to each other and pray for each other so that you may be healed. The prayer of a righteous man is powerful and effective."[1]

Forgiveness is one of those "day-to-day" things that we need to work on to experience the full freedom Jesus brought us, because internal healing takes place when we confess our mistakes and request forgiveness. This leads to power in our day-to-day lives as God is unleashed to do greater things through us.

To get this kind of healing requires honest confession—not the popular weenie kind that goes something like, "If I offended you in any way, I'm sorry." Did you see Jim Carey's *Liar Liar*? In that movie the main character suffers an ailment in which he inexplicably tells the brutal truth instead of the half-truths he was accustomed to. Well, when we use the line "... in any way" it's a half-truth. What we really mean is, "I'm sorry that you found out what I did, and I'm sorry that it is going to affect our relationship in a way that might hurt my

1. James 5:16.

interests. So in order to get you off my back and do damage control, I'm going to say something that makes me look humble and sorrowful when I'm really not."

There are a lot of people I wouldn't enjoy meeting in the store—or anywhere. But I'm thankful to say that there is no interaction I'm dreading to have. There is no information that I'm dreading someone else will find out. It *is* possible to have a clear conscience—and that's an important cog in the wheel of freedom.[2]

To be clear, I have done a lot of dreadful things. I've cheated in school (and then blew up the mailbox of the teacher who caught me). I've stolen money from the church I used to work for. I've . . . well, I think I've confessed enough in this forum. You don't need me to keep going.

I've also sought to confess my sin to the people I've wronged and to the best of my ability make the situation right. To give you a couple of examples of how this could look, here are two confession letters I wrote to people I wronged.

The first letter is one I sent to the current pastor of the church where I worked for eight years. I also sent a copy to the pastor who, at the time, was an authority over me:

> *Dear Bob,*
>
> *A few days ago, in a time of prayer, the Lord brought to my mind a sin that I felt led to confess to you as the pastor of North Park Church. Though this sin was committed under someone else's watch, it was a sin against the church, which is now under*

2. Acts 24:16; 1 Corinthians 4:4; 2 Corinthians 1:12.

your leadership. Please receive this confession and feel free to take whatever step you feel appropriate.

When I was the youth pastor during the years 1987 to 1990, I would collect money for various weekend trips. Often kids would give me cash, which would then sit in an envelope in the lower left-hand drawer of my desk. At that point in my life, I was very deficient in areas relating to administration. Therefore the envelope would sit for weeks until I would remember to turn it in to the money counters.

By this time the bookkeeper would have already written checks to the appropriate camps or vendors. When the money would finally get turned in, it would almost always reflect less than the total combined costs for the trip. That was because there always was at least one kid who received some sort of "scholarship." This was within my authority; so far so good.

However, there were a few times when I was short on my own personal cash and needed to get some lunch. At times I would dip into the envelope with the intention of paying it back whenever I was able to make it to the ATM. Unfortunately, there were times when the money was never repaid, and the result was that I stole from the church and from the Lord. I had ways to rationalize this. This was nothing more than deeper levels of sin and rationalization.

It has been many years since I have asked God to forgive my sin. I believed He did. However, I've always had the nagging thought of the need to make restitution and confess to a person in leadership at the church. Just today, in a time of extended reflection and confession, I realized that I had to do this in order to bring biblical closure.

I estimate that I probably stole around $100 total. This is a very, very rough estimate, and it could be wrong, but I think it is on *the high side. I've chosen to double the amount. What I ask of you is the following: (1.) Consider forgiving me on behalf of the leadership of NPC. If you feel a need to take this beyond yourself, that is completely up to you, and I will respect that and wait for your response. And (2.) accept the $200 check for restitution relating to my sin. If you want more, name the amount.*

Bob, sorry for complicating your life and ministry with this letter. I humbly ask for your forgiveness. Please let me know if there is anything more I can do for you or the church.

In His Grip,

Brian Tome

Next is a confession and offer of restitution to one of my high school teachers:

Dear Mr. Hurleywine,

I don't know if you remember me. Unfortunately, you probably do. My name is Brian Tome. I had you for chemistry in the eleventh grade. During a test you flipped a student handbook onto my desk with the section on cheating highlighted in red. You saw me with a cheat sheet and chose to give me an F for the semester.

Being a rebellious and vengeful person, I chose to blow up your mailbox with an M-80. That was unacceptable behavior on my part, for which I am very sorry.

Going into my senior year, I chose to move from being a churchgoer to becoming a Christ-follower (Christian). I recognized what I had done as sin and asked God for forgiveness. However, I always felt deep inside that this wasn't good enough. I needed to ask you for forgiveness and make restitution. That is the purpose of this communication.

Partly due to cowardice and partly due to forgetfulness, it has taken me twenty years to take this step. I ask that you would forgive me for the stress, discomfort, and even trauma I may have caused you and your family in destroying your personal property. Enclosed is a check for $100 that I hope covers the cost of the mailbox plus a little interest. If this is unacceptable, please let me know.

Mr. Hurleywine, please feel free to contact me if you feel it is necessary. Also, if there is anything else I can do to make this situation right, I'd like to know. Please forgive me for sinning against you and God.

> *In His Grip,*
> *Brian Tome*

Those letters and the checks were hard to write. But it seems that right now in the stage I'm at, some hard things are bringing me growth and advancement. Freedom isn't cheap. *Talk* is cheap. If you want forgiveness and its ensuing freedom, you need to show it. This means that as much as you are able, you need to try to right the wrong. If you stole money, it should be returned with the interest it could have earned. If you slandered a person's reputation, don't just ask forgiveness. Call *every* person involved and tell the truth—maybe take out a full-page ad in the local newspaper. If you cheated and obtained a reward or honor, return it.

When you really want forgiveness, you won't necessarily want restitution, but you will be willing to go through with it after some wrestling, because freedom is precious and healing. So when you want integrity, you'll go after it hard. We can see this at numerous places in the Bible, and here's one example: "Many of those who believed now came and openly confessed their evil deeds. A number who had practiced sorcery brought their scrolls together and burned them publicly. When they calculated the value of the scrolls, the total came to fifty thousand drachmas."[3]

A drachma was a silver coin worth about a day's wages. These followers of Christ realized they needed to burn the cause of the offense, so they did restitution in the amount of fifty thousand days' worth of paychecks. You might say, "That's insane! Who would do that?" Someone who has integrity, who wants healing, and who has truly experienced God. (If you aren't getting this, you aren't getting God either.) These people said, "I have a relationship with God. I've experienced His love through His only Son, Jesus Christ. I must turn away from the spoils of my previous, warped way of living."

The process of getting this kind of freedom is also called repentance—turning from the way we are going and heading in the direction of God and His ways. He says, "I, even I, am he who blots out your transgressions, for my own sake, and remembers your sins no more."[4] So God—the same One who rescues us from the auction block—takes our repented sins into a time capsule that will never be found and will never get in the way of His love for us. That, friends, is freedom.

---

3. Acts 19:18–19.
4. Isaiah 43:25 TNIV.

Part 2: Giving Forgiveness

I too often assume that when I've been hurt by someone, he or she was intentionally trying to dishonor my reputation or bring me harm. So much of our pain would vanish or would never take root if we just said to ourselves, "They didn't mean it that way. They didn't know. I'm sure they were just thinking about something else when that happened."

The best thing you can do to keep from being hurt is to assume that people's intentions were pure and that they didn't mean what they said or did. Quit jumping to conclusions.

My first (freeing) strategy when dealing with pain is to mark it down—not as in writing it down, but deeply discounting it as if it was in the clearance bin for a year. In fact, I discount the experiences so deeply that they aren't worth anything. Here are some examples of how to discount things and get free.

- "A man's wisdom gives him patience; it is to his glory to overlook an offense."[5]
- "A fool shows his annoyance at once, but a prudent man overlooks an insult."[6]
- "My dear brothers, take note of this: Everyone should be quick to listen, slow to speak, and slow to become angry."[7]

5. Proverbs 19:11.
6. Proverbs 12:16.
7. James 1:19.

So much of our hurt would be eliminated—so much of our bondage released—if we could simply learn on the front end to overlook offenses and be slow to anger.

And I need to take my own advice, because I'm stewing right now. I made the mistake of checking my e-mail last night before I went to bed. I got a message accusing me of making a move that wasn't filled with integrity. A few different times in the e-mail I could hear the sarcastic, disdainful tone in the person's heart as the person typed, "Tell me you didn't just . . . blah blah blah!"

I worked all night on my response—not with my fingers on the keyboard, but with my head on the pillow. Finally, I got up in the morning and tried to have some time with God. I wanted to read and concentrate on the authorized biography of Jesus according to Matthew. Instead, I found myself continuing to craft my response in my head.

Then I realized I might as well stop trying to talk with God and just write the e-mail. So for fifteen minutes I was having a great time. My fingers were blazing as my face was grimacing. I was vicariously talking to the screen the way I would never talk to this person's face. It was fun. Here's my opening line:

Dear Jerk Face,

Wow. I want to say, "Thank you for your feedback" . . . but not this time. Tell me you aren't assuming the worst in me!

It only gets juicier from there, but here's the strange thing: five minutes after typing various vengeful lines, I felt no better. It's morbidly fun in the moment, but it doesn't last. Morbid fun never leads to freedom. The longer I fixate on how I perceive myself to have been wronged, the more bondage I experience. I'm not free to enjoy life or learn about God. Instead, I'm bound to figure out how to get even and make that person feel the way he or she has made me feel.

Having vengeful fantasies is as productive as eating rat poison. Keep munching on Rat Zapper and it'll put you six feet under. Likewise, you'll spiritually die if you continue to munch on the bitterness of your perceived wrongs. Now, I say "perceived" wrongs because oftentimes we don't see reality when we're stewing and grimacing and hurting. Before I responded to "Jerk Face," I forwarded my e-mail to some trusted friends with whom I have community—just to do the checks and balance—because there are numerous times where my perception doesn't match reality. I don't want to send an inflammatory e-mail if I've read into things that weren't said. Sure enough, my friends told me that I was imagining things that weren't said and maybe weren't even implied.

Okay, but maybe you're asking, "What about the wrongs that aren't perceived but are bona fide? What about when I've been fired for an unjust cause or passed over for the promotion because the other person lied about his contribution to a project? What if I was abused as a child or gossiped about? In those situations aren't we justified in a measured vengeful response?"

No. "Do not take revenge, my friends, but leave room for God's wrath, for it is written: 'It is mine to avenge; I will repay,' says the Lord."[8] I know this is hard to swallow, but unless you're a governing official who is commissioned to enact justice on behalf of society, nowhere in your job description is the need to avenge. That's exclusively in God's job description—and it's for our own good. Seriously. Not only does it not work when we take matters into our own hands, but we lose our freedom by putting ourselves in bondage to emotions such as suspicion, hate, paranoia, and bitterness. Or we're simply maniacally working to prove the offending party wrong. That's an exhausting way to live.

Your dad told you that you will never amount to anything, and even though you are earning more than you thought you would at this stage of the game, you still think about those words and they prompt your unhealthy work ethic. Your spouse made a comment about your appearance before you were even married, and you still feel you can't measure up—even though apologies have been made. A previous boss said that you didn't have the ability to run with the big dogs, and that comment still propels you to prove her wrong. All these tightly held wrongs have created areas in our lives that interfere with our freedom.

Of course, if you are genuinely hurt and the pain isn't going away, you can't just sit and deny that you are hurt. I'm not saying to be stoic and ignore your pain. If you do, your neighbors will one day be seen on the eleven o'clock news saying, "He was such a quiet man," in response to the fact that you used a tommy gun to mow down people at a bus stop. No, we have

8. Romans 12:19.

to deal with our hurts instead of denying our hurts so that we don't have to live up to the cliché that says, "Hurt people hurt people." Instead, realize you are hurt and take steps to recover from your pain—not vengeful steps like praying for God to hurt your enemy or trying to crush a person's reputation, but healthy steps of prayer, trusted counsel, and release.

Jesus regularly practiced and taught freedom through forgiveness because His friends didn't fully understand how forgiveness could be practiced without some sort of vengeance. Once, in order to make sure he wasn't misunderstanding Jesus, Peter asked, "Lord, how many times shall I forgive my brother when he sins against me? Up to seven times?" Jesus answered, "I tell you, not seven times, but seventy-seven times."[9]

For most of us, forgiveness happens only when conditions are perfect. Here's a typical forgiveness fantasy: the person who has hurt us is somehow smitten with sorrow and comes to us, tearful and groveling on their knees, saying, "Ooooohhhh, I'm such a wicked, vile worm with bad breath. I have sinned against God, against humanity, and against you and the horse you rode in on. I am sooooo sorrrrrrrrry. I don't deserve anything from a person as great and noble as you. But can you find it anywhere in your pure heart to forgive me? Please forgive me. Pretty please?" Then we say in return, "Well . . . that's okay. I forgive you, but don't do it again!" If that happens, it's a beautiful thing. But Jesus can't be referring to that type of fantasy scenario. There is no way that can happen seventy-seven times or even seven times. I mean, how often has that

9. Matthew 18:21–22.

happened for you? Those are protracted and lengthy conversations that no one has the time and energy for on a consistent basis. (And most people never admit to bad breath.)

Though it's very healthy, ideal, and easy for the offender to come and offer apologies, it is not the only God-honoring way to experience forgiveness and bounce back from hurt. If it were, none of us would recover from our hurt and be restored to wholeness.

In the last few years, I've been hurt more than ever before in my life. The people who have hurt me the most have never come to me and said one word—other than that everything is my problem. But for me to keep my freedom, I've had to practice the kind of forgiveness that Jesus practiced and taught—the kind that doesn't depend on anyone ever asking for forgiveness. One passage that slapped me into shape is this one: "'Forgive us our debts, as we also have forgiven our debtors. And lead us not into temptation, but deliver us from the evil one.' For if you forgive men when they sin against you, your heavenly Father will also forgive you. But if you do not forgive men their sins, your Father will not forgive your sins."[10]

The word for "forgive" that Jesus uses here and other places is translated from the Greek word *aphiemi*. According to the *Theological Dictionary of the New Testament*, which is the most respected Greek epistemological scholarly work currently published, it means "to send off," or "to let go," or "to let be."[11] In other words, "to be free."

10. Matthew 6:12–15.
11. G. Kittel, G. W. Bromiley, and G. Friedrich, eds., *Theological Dictionary of the New Testament*, vols. 5–9, 10 (Grand Rapids: Eerdmans, 1964–c1976), CD-ROM.

Jesus is saying that when we pray, we must have regular times when we release our claim against other people who have hurt us. Instead of banishing them to a corner of our brain set aside for those we hate, we should instead release those thoughts. Rather than putting them in a sort of prison where they have to munch Rat Zapper 24/7, we need to send them away. In doing so, we are giving them freedom. Here's the amazing part: *the way we become free is by enabling other people to become free.*

At first glance, it sounds as though Jesus is saying that God withholds our forgiveness until we forgive other people. The problem with strictly adhering to that interpretation is that it is against the grain of grace. If Jesus waited to give us something until we had given Him something first, we would be getting a paycheck from Him, not grace. God doesn't withhold what we need until we obey.

I think God's economy of freedom is relative to relationships: our relationship with Him and our relationships with others. The more we give forgiveness, the easier it will be for us to receive forgiveness from God. The more we receive forgiveness from God, the easier it will be to give forgiveness to others. Staying free means I go with the flow of forgiveness.

I know some people who have a very hard time believing that God has forgiven them for their mistakes (or what the Lord's Prayer calls "trespasses," "sins," or "debts"). They can't believe that God can truly release His right to take vengeance for our sexual trysts, business bankruptcies, and general spiritual rebellion. So, in turn, these folks have a hard time releasing other people when they could take vengeance.

Instead of forgiving those who wrong them, they keep swallowing the endless supply of bitter pills—even though a big dose of *aphiemi* is the remedy.

Likewise, I know people who find it pretty easy to forgive the person who borrowed their property, damaged it, and never paid for it. These people receive grace from God pretty freely for the way they ding themselves up by disobeying God's laws.

Since the word Jesus uses for forgiveness means "let go," "send away," or "tolerate," instead of bitterly storing up our grievances in our minds and waiting for some sort of official forgiveness scenario, Jesus is promoting the value of saying to oneself and to God, "I need to be done with this attitude and with this pain. I need to offer it up and release it." In doing so we are released of the grudge and on the way to experiencing fuller freedom. So if you want to be free—both in God's eyes and in your emotions toward others—you must learn to release your grievances.

Here's a short list of some of my own things I could bitterly store up—or things I had stored up but then released by choosing, instead, to extend grace:

- being given up for adoption by my birth parents;
- bouncing checks to buy gifts for my close friends in college, only to be the last to leave the party and see nearly all of them left on the floor, discarded and damaged;
- a friend spreading rumors that I'd cheated on my wife, when the truth is that the only woman I've ever been with is my wife, Libby;

- releasing staff members for immoral behavior only to have other churches hire them without a reference check;
- feeling my kids don't notice or appreciate the great life that is afforded them;
- long-time attendees at our church living off the gratitude of generous givers while refusing to sacrifice for the benefit of others;
- being accused of sexual harassment.

I used to struggle with the idea that God forgets our sins. How can that be? Does He have dementia? Is it really a good thing that God forgets? A business owner shouldn't forget about an employee's embezzlement; otherwise he may put the same person in the same position and create more damage. But it's not the same with God.

To forget sin doesn't mean we shouldn't make adjustments. If a babysitter violates your child, don't "forgive and forget" by hiring him or her again. But in order for you to be free, you must release that burden and bitterness. So forgetting means intentionally releasing and putting an offense out of your mind and choosing to not inflict damage on the offender. You can still participate in a legal process—governing authorities are set up for such matters. However, be wary of whether you are participating in truth or simply fueling bitterness.

I'm also not talking about reconciling the relationship by having it go on as it always did—because that's not always the right thing. If reconciliation is the right thing, it will take two people. Forgiveness takes one.

I don't go around with the offenses listed above on my mind. I've literally freed and released these wrongs. In fact, going over this manuscript prior to print I remember again that I had forgotten these things—meaning, I'm free from their negative effects. I have to work to bring them up, because I have given up my perceived right to exact payment from these people. I could have given the names of everyone above, and then thousands of people would know how dirty they were. Actually, that sounds like fun. In fact, it's even fun for me to type this as a possibility. I can sense the taste of rat poison on my lips just considering it. I can also take vengeance by thinking bad, hate-filled thoughts against them. In doing this I am trying to bind them up, but really I'm just putting myself in prison. Maybe this is a part of why Jesus says that to hate someone is like murdering someone.[12] Both acts begin with bitterness and end with bondage. Freedom cannot exist where hate or murder are present.

I was recently in South Africa with a group of people, and as is often the case when a team gets outside of America into strange territory, a bonding took place—a bonding with one another and with God. This was apparent each evening as we debriefed our experiences of that day, which included loving on AIDS patients, giving shoes to the shoeless, and receiving love from our friends at Charity and Faith Mission Church.

One evening a woman named Jen opened up about the difficulty she had growing up in a dysfunctional family with an alcoholic mother. Her family life was not easy and is still

12. Matthew 5:22; 1 John 3:15.

not easy. She tearfully told us of how her mother would bad-mouth her father and regularly get drunk and pass out in the bathroom, requiring Jen to step over her in order to brush her teeth. She recounted that when her dad died her mom refused to be a part of the funeral. Jen raised her younger siblings and buried her dad alone. Life just isn't supposed to operate that way.

The next day we were on a bus off to our next assignment. Jen sat in a seat behind me with another woman on a long and bumpy ride. For the majority of that ride, Jen recounted even further painful slights at the hand of her mother. At first I grieved for her, but then something clicked. When we got off the bus, I pulled Jen aside and humbly and tentatively offered up a leading question: "Do you want to be free of the pain and bitterness that your mother has given you?"

She said yes.

"Then you can never talk about this again. No more 'processing' or 'venting.' You've been through counseling and have talked this to death. Every time you talk about it again, you are reliving all the experiences and taking on all the pain in a renewed way."

In my previous book, *Welcome to the Revolution*, I wrote about the blessing of the mind and how imagination is a powerful multimedia tool in communicating with God. Likewise, the mind is a powerful tool to relive pain and re-create fresh wounds. So I challenged Jen to talk only about past situations regarding her mother in two contexts: when she prays and when she gets on the other side of pain as a tool to help someone else be free. This was her only hope for freedom. The years of counseling, venting, and processing had run their course. It was time to pull out an unconventional weapon: praying for and blessing her enemies. This is what Jesus did when hanging on a cross. He said, "Father, forgive them, for they do not know what they are doing."[13] Jesus forgave without someone officially asking forgiveness from Him.

Stephen was the first person ever martyred for his faith in Jesus. As he was being stoned, he said to God, "Lord, do not hold this sin against them."[14] Can you imagine? That's intense forgiveness.

You may be saying, "I can't do this. It hurts too much." You are hurting right now. Do you think it is going to get any better? What do you really have to lose? Start giving it a try by praying this prayer right now.

> *God, I'm not sure I understand what it means to forgive, let alone how to forgive. But, I do know that I don't want to be fixated on my pain any longer. I'm in bondage, and I don't like it. I want to learn how to get over the injustices that have been done to me. I want to enjoy life and enjoy You. Right now that isn't possible. Please help me learn how to forgive _____ for _____. I want to be free.*

When you ask for freedom, you will receive it. Jen did pray for her mom and now she is released from that burden. You can experience the same thing.

---

13. Luke 23:34 TNIV.
14. Acts 7:60.

Chapter 6 ———

Strongholds

I used to joke that I was the most effective counselor anyone would ever need. I offered a counseling trifecta of three sessions with three words each. After hearing the story, session one was "Deal with it." Session two was "Get over it." If change hadn't taken root, then in the third session I would say, "Get a life!" While I never literally performed a counseling trifecta, I did believe that moving on from hurts, problems, addictions, and hang-ups should be that simple. Years later, with more life experience and reflection on the core message in the Bible, I now know that isn't true. I now know there is a much more sinister and persuasive power that is trying to keep us in bondage. It is not as simple as "getting over it."

There are things that aren't visible to the eye but still spiritually control or limit us, and they're called strongholds. Like the military term used to describe a place that's well fortified and defended, strongholds are intentionally or unintentionally built around areas in our lives that block us from experiencing the fullness of freedom. Sometimes we think strongholds will provide security and freedom—sometimes we're not even aware of them—but ultimately they never deliver.

Strongholds are the reason why some of us don't trust any authority figure; we think they're all twisted. We think our manager is out to get us, that all pastors and priests are wacked, that police only eat jelly doughnuts and discriminate. We envy each other and want what others have. We don't speak up in conversations because we think we'll be judged or mocked. We're worried that the guy in the next cubical will get ahead faster. We're so nervous about picking the right spouse that we don't date, or we see one flaw in a potential mate and run. Or we're so nervous about deciphering God's "calling" that we get fixed in one spot and don't have the guts to move. These fears are strongholds, but they are ones we can overcome.

Fear defines us, walls us off, and blocks us from healthy relationships with others and with God. Most of us think our fears are normal. We trick our brains into believing we're just being responsible, good planners or typical, healthy competitors.

Some of you reading this book are thinking, *I don't have these strongholds. I'm not fearful; I'm just responsible.* Or you're thinking, *I'm not fearful; I'm just being reasonable based on my past experiences.* Yet any thought that keeps you from doing something that Jesus would do is based on a stronghold of fear, and not reasoning that comes from faith.

If you want to experience fear cloaked in "reason," take a trip to a foreign country for purposes other than getting a tan. In the past few years, I've been to South Africa, Israel, and Nicaragua. In all situations I had plenty of conversations with "reasonable" people who thought I was making a mistake. When heading to South Africa, we were told we'd either get AIDS as soon as we got off the plane or that white people in exclusively black townships invite rape and riots. When we went to Israel the stay-at-homers felt we were going to get the bird flu or get bombed. In Nicaragua the fear was that a political rebellion would break out and we wouldn't get back home. Since we think America is the home of the brave, we don't want to go to any country that can't ensure us 100 percent safety.

Sally Neubauer, my mother-in-law, went on a mission trip to Russia just after the cold war ended. A healthy, strapping thirty-year-old friend of mine had paid for his ticket and was also ready to go. Then his average American friends and family got a hold of him. They convinced him it was too dangerous. He didn't go. Even though he looked physically strong, he was a spiritual weenie boy. My aged, Birkenstock-wearing mother-in-law exhibited a spirit of God's power and love, whereas my friend showed timidity and fear.

The look I saw on this guy's face when Sally came back and shared her experiences and victories (and even the ruts she hit) is the same look I saw on the faces of those people who tried to talk me out of going to South Africa and Israel: it said, *I wish I had gone too.* Well, guess what? You still can. You can go to places where God's Spirit compels you to go (and I'll talk more about that Spirit in the next few chapters). These are places of power and love. But first you must discipline yourself to notice your strongholds and fight against them.

I had just finished talking about strongholds to a group of two hundred people who were headed to South Africa. Twenty-four hours earlier a guy on the team that went over ahead of time was carjacked at gunpoint. Some poverty-stricken South Africans made him get out of his truck as they drove off with bountiful supplies. He decided to blog about the event, and so fear was running rampant among many who were about to depart on the plane. The entire team needed encouragement to break their strongholds of fear, which could have robbed them of being a blessing to the community they were headed to and also of receiving blessings themselves. Thankfully, they all followed through and experienced invigorating freedom.

Usually we build strongholds as a way to protect ourselves, but in reality they paralyze and keep us isolated. We can break free of strongholds, but first we have to identify them.[1] Here are some marks of strongholds:

1. *You have repeated, unwanted behavior.* You might do things you don't want to do, or fail to do the things you really want to do. Or maybe you're continuing to do something that you just know deep down isn't right. This can range from drinking six beers every night to constantly criticizing and assuming the worst of people.

2. *You have memory gaps.* If you can't go back and recall several crisp memories from a specific period of your life, it's likely that something took place during that time that is defining who you are. You just chalk it up to a bad memory, but my guess is that something is walling you in. If you don't have vivid memories from the years you were growing up—your school classroom, the house you grew up in, and so on—maybe something negative or painful happened in one of those places and you've blocked that time and place in your mind. If so, that old scenario is affecting your life right now.

1. 2 Corinthians 10:4.

3. **You have confusion as to "why."** You see yourself do something, say something, defend yourself in a certain way, and you don't know why you regularly respond the way you do. But you know you don't like it.

4. **There's something about you that no one knows.** Think about when you're playing that icebreaker game, "Tell us something we don't know about you." There's generally someone who can't answer—he just gets stuck—because he knows the perfect answer to that question but will never say it. Or you have "family secrets" that you learned as a child were always inappropriate to tell anybody. And that's the thing molding your heart.

5. **You have bitterness toward a person or type of person.** You don't like men, women, cops, Republicans, Iranians, white people, GE Customer Service representatives— whoever. It's habitual and generic. You know nothing about that person, but you're bitter because of something or someone she or he is aligned with. You refuse to give that person the benefit of the doubt.

6. **You blindly accept your limitations.** "That's just the way I am," you say, and brush it off. For instance, I've heard people with an Irish heritage dismiss their angry outbursts with "It's because I'm Irish." I've heard Italians dismiss their sexual escapades because "It's just what we do." I've heard South Africans dismiss their inability to honor other people's schedules by showing up on time because they're on "South African time" and people who always retreat say, "I'm French" (just kidding . . . but it was funny). You may have been painted as critical, harsh, selfish, flaky,

insensitive, vain, insecure, mealy-mouthed, aloof, or weak-willed years ago, and at some point you believed it and just let it describe you from then on. To blindly accept our quirks and lapses is exactly the purpose of a stronghold.

Going through this list, let's just admit that we're all in bondage to something and we're not experiencing full freedom. Even now I'm realizing some of my bondage. For instance, I have the repeated, unwanted behavior of being competitive. Let's say I'm around someone who drives a BMW and I pull up in my old minivan. I'll competitively think, *I might not have a good car, but I definitely give away more money than he does.* It's embarrassing to admit, but that's the truth about me. My competitive streak can get me into ugly places instead of staying on the basketball court where it belongs.

It might take a little while to figure out your strongholds. It might take you asking some other people who spend plenty of time with you and are willing to speak the hard truth to help point them out in you. Ask a simple question like, "Is there anything you see in me that you think I don't see in me?" or "Is there anything you see me regularly doing that makes you wonder why I do it?" or "If you were me for a day, what would you change?" Then sit back and receive what they say with grace.

Understand that whatever you are going to hear will probably hurt. The person you ask for help probably won't answer in the precise way he or she should. But this is not an exercise for the other person to communicate beautifully; it's about you receiving beautifully. He or she is talking about an area that has a grip on you. What that person has to say may make you recoil—you might try not to receive. It may help to preemptively apologize for how you will respond, but assure the person that you really want to hear the truth and that you know God put him or her in your life for a reason. Give it a shot.

The unfortunate thing about strongholds is that they can be established suddenly, get deeply rooted in no time, and last until you *intentionally* face them (and you'll probably have to face them consistently). Have you been through things that were painful or simply wrong? Now they define, limit, or blind you. You've never experienced true grace? Now you resist telling the truth. Instead of protecting yourself and getting out from under the stronghold, you just live with it. Maybe you've even grown to like it.

Strongholds are hard to break, even after you've identified them. Dark spiritual personalities love when you're running on a treadmill and you bump up your speed to match the guy's next to you (even if he's fifty pounds lighter). The dark personalities love when you believe you need to buy more and more so people admire your possessions. They love when you can't let go of the comment someone once made about your big nose—and no matter how much plastic surgery you have, you think you can't measure up. Or you say to yourself, "My husband lied to me once, and I can never trust him again." All that is bondage, because it's untrue. Your treadmill speed is just fine. Your nose is fine. Your wardrobe is fine. You can rebuild trust with your husband or wife. But those spiritual personalities are out there plotting and strengthening your stronghold's false view of reality. They're excited that you relive your abuse over and over, or that you can't even remember the abuse but something about your behavior is unnatural and you can't experience the intimacy God intended you to enjoy with the person you married. The evil ones love that. They love your self-destruction because they authored it in the first place.

Some strongholds can actually serve us well for a period of time, but what began as positive can later sour. One such stronghold could be called the "spirit of performance." Yes, following Jesus includes diligence, but thinking that our diligent performance is part of our core identity or a way to earn brownie points will eventually put us in bondage.

A friend of mine, Dora, dealt with this. She struggled with continual thoughts of feeling rejected and needing to "perform" for attention and acceptance. Performing for her began to look like acting like she wasn't hurt or upset when she actually was. She pushed hard in her corporate career, and even things that should have been leisure activities became moments to perform and pass some sort of grade—hoping to earn God's approval and the approval of others.

When you struggle with any stronghold, including this one, you lose the freedom to express your true self. For Dora this meant she developed an outer shell and personality that was "tough." All her relationships became difficult because strongholds don't do well with intimacy. The crazy thing is that as feminine as Dora is right now, when she was under the power of the stronghold, you wouldn't have known it. She wore "manly" clothes. She viewed femininity as weak and rejected the desire to be a mother. She actually loved being seen as unapproachable and tough.

Then Jesus broke in and helped her see that this persona was fabricated and not the real her. God started working in her life and showing her places He wanted to bring healing. Meeting her husband and accepting his tender teaching—and sometimes rebuking—was a huge part of that process.

Eventually Dora uncovered that the reason she was all about performance was that at her core she felt rejected. When she realized that the hard outer shell of performance was a coping mechanism, she could grab the antidote: receiving Jesus and His love.

Now, just as it took a long time for the nation of Israel to truly experience the fullness of freedom when Charlton Heston—I mean Moses—led them out of slavery, Dora still has to pay attention to her attitudes and choices and work through this arduous process. When she's in the gym, she notices that she still has the tendency to peek at the treadmill beside her to measure her running performance against that of the person next to her. Even though she wants to speed up, she instead chooses to get off the treadmill entirely so she doesn't give in to the temptation to outperform. It takes daily grunt work. And in doing the work, she's not giving the enemy a "foothold" that would lead to losing more freedom.[2]

These are the kinds of things we have to do to experience the peace of freedom. Breaking strongholds—which is a process we'll explore in a little more detail next—can be exhausting, but once you gain freedom, you won't want to be anywhere else.

2. Ephesians 4:27.

Do you see why someone had to set us free—and has to set us free over and over again? Jesus is the Freedom Creator and ultimate Stronghold Breaker, and that's not just a one-time deal. He's the Savior when you first come to Him with your need, and He's the Savior every day you need to be set free and reminded of who you are and how life can be lived in freedom. He broke through the stronghold of death, and nothing is more difficult. He left the grave and thereby created a new system of freedom for us. It is for me; it is for you.

So what do we do with our strongholds? We uncover them first, whether that comes by asking people we trust to point them out, or just taking a hard, honest look at our lives and asking God to reveal them to us. (He will if you ask. "In my anguish I cried to the LORD, and he answered by setting me free."[3]) Once you figure them out, it's about moving forward. Strongholds are numerous, so depending on what yours are, it might require some good counseling, people to be accountable to, and possibly a new community. And really, we can't deal with them all at once. Life is a process, and being freed by Jesus is a process too. Just as the nation of Israel went through a process in being freed from Egypt and having the full fruits of freedom, so also strongholds are eliminated in your life through a process that requires patience. Deal with the stage you are in and *then* move on to the next one. It will definitely require that you talk through your strongholds with God, continue to talk through them, and do the daily grunt work of breaking free.

3. Psalm 118:5.

Chapter 7

The Spirit World

The strongholds we've been talking about aren't "tests" from God. He's not waiting to see if you'll sink or swim. We all sink, we all swim, and we all need God, who wants us all to be absolutely fulfilled so we can live the adventurous life of following Him.

However, a multi-pronged problem keeps us from being free; it's not just petty fears, lack of forgiveness, and past pains that hold us back. It's also present spiritual forces. We don't talk about this stuff very often, and many times those who do aren't exactly like the guys we're hanging out with on the weekend. But we need to take a serious and sober look at a reality that is affecting us whether we recognize it or not.

God wants your life to be great. But great things are often thwarted by unseen things. I reflected on this while reading about the creation of the Panama Canal in David McCullough's *Path Between the Seas*. The major problem in thwarting the progress of that great project was the number of workers who kept falling ill and dying from malaria and yellow fever. When an out-of-the-box doctor surmised that mosquitos carried and transferred disease, people laughed.

In the hospital wards, nurses placed the four legs of each bed in four pots of water. This was thought to create a moat which spiders and rats wouldn't cross. Instead it created a perfect breeding ground for assassins who carried germs. Many of our seemingly good and reasonable ideas and convictions are breeding grounds for negative spiritual personalities who inflict spiritual disease.

There are personalities—specific ones—in the spiritual realm who draw us into places of fear, immobility, and ultimately bondage. These personalities want to blind us to our freedom and keep the bondage tight. Not only do these forces dissuade us from heaven, but they're also just as interested in keeping us in bondage here on earth. The Bible calls these personalities "demons" or "evil spirits," and they intend to steal life from you. True life. Eternal life.

Eternal life is eternal freedom, and it starts the moment God's Spirit (sometimes referred to as the Holy Ghost) inhabits us. We don't have to wait until heaven, though, to find freedom. (Or maybe I should say, we don't have to wait until we die to experience the freedom and fullness of heaven.) So whenever we're feeling restriction and bondage—whether it's because of fear, abuse of authority, self-imposed limitations, poor choices, unclear vision, or flat-out demonic oppression—it's because we have an enemy who wants the worst for us.

Okay, name this TV show: "Yeah, and I would have gotten away with it too, if it weren't for those meddling kids!" If you are an American under the age of fifty and had parents who let you watch cartoons, you know the answer: *Scooby-Doo.*

Scooby, Shaggy, and the rest of the neck-scarf–wearing gang spent each episode exploring various buildings while being chased by ghosts. But they always solved the mystery and realized that it wasn't a ghost after all—something would fall on the ghost, like a bucket of water, and partially disrobe him. They'd discover that all along it had been Old Man McStupid pretending to be a ghost with a pirate hat and king-sized sheet. At the end of the show the bad guys were always apprehended as they muttered their standard line, still dripping water, "Yeah, and we would have gotten away with it, too, if it weren't for those pesky kids!"

The day *Scooby-Doo* ceased to be scary was the day you realized the ghost was always a hoax. And ghost hoaxes still happen today. Sometimes the "paranormal" gets proven to be nothing more than a unique circumstance explained through scientific methods. No matter how many ghost myths get busted, though, most of us are never completely going to stop believing in ghosts and other paranormal phenomenon. If you believe in a spirit realm, there's nothing I could tell you to make you stop believing. That's because most of us have experienced something science can't explain. Or someone intelligent and well grounded whom you trust has told you about an experience with the spirit realm, and you aren't ready to call that person delusional or a liar.

If you haven't experienced something from the spirit realm or don't know someone who has, then I at least know this: you want to believe. I'm not talking about the *Scooby-Doo* brand of ghost. I'm talking about something outside the physical world that helps you make sense out of your physical world. You hope there is a spirit realm. If you're an average person, you wake up in the morning having had a memorably graphic dream and wonder if God was sending you a sign.

Maybe you walked into a dark room and thought something was there or naturally hoped something wasn't there. We are physical, but at the same time we are incurably spiritual.

Please don't be freaked out by this. This revelation (if it is one) shouldn't cause you any more consternation than when you learned there is such a thing as a flu bug. The flu bug has always been there whether you felt its ill effects or saw it with your naked eye or not. Likewise, your awareness and education surrounding negative spiritual personalities doesn't make evil any more powerful or influential in your life. In fact, this should be a liberating revelation for you.

Some people think that if we just ignore the spiritual "mumbo jumbo" stuff we don't understand, then it just doesn't exist and will somehow leave us alone. Those same people assume that if you get involved in the reality of the spiritual world (i.e., start talking to God about this stuff, recognizing and calling it out in the world around you, and participating in the spiritual reality), then the creepy spiritual powers-that-be will find you and start messing with you more. That is definitely not the case. When Jesus was encouraging people to receive God's Holy Ghost, He said, "Which of you fathers, if your son asks for a fish, will give him a snake instead?"[1] The Bible often uses fish as a metaphor for God's provision, so the idea here is that if you're asking God for truth, freedom, and His words, then He's not going to let you get burned by evil spirits ("a snake") as a result. If the spiritual world is a reality, God doesn't want you ignorant of it or attempting to flee from

1. Luke 11:11.

it. And I'm sure you know, deep down, that you don't want to be ignorant of it either.

Have you ever noticed how many books on the best-seller lists are spiritual or religious in content? It's ironic, because many infamous scholars and top thinkers believed that as the world in general (and the Western world, in particular) became more educated, belief in a transcendent world would vanish. Yet much of our reading diet continues to consist of subjects of a nonphysical and unscientific nature—subjects that can't be put in a test tube or empirically charted on a spreadsheet.

Much of what is in the Bible can't be scientifically measured. For this reason Voltaire said that the Bible would be entirely discredited and out of print before the end of his life. As we become more educated, Voltaire thought, we'll become less interested in the spiritual. And yet, today, even as knowledge has increased exponentially in the more than 200 years after Voltaire's death (and as the Bible continues to vastly outsell the works of Voltaire, many of which are out of print), people aren't less interested in the spiritual. Clearly it's the opposite.

When we're faced with a physical problem the doctors can't solve, we automatically turn to prayer or some sort of calling out. When we wake up after a nightmare, we wonder if evil forces are really trying to get us. When we get in a car accident and feel dramatically shaken, we assume God is trying to tell us something. Why is it that when things go bump in the night the hair on the backs of our necks stands up? Why the fascination with psychics, astrology, and all sorts of mystical paraphernalia—even though we realize that much (or maybe even all) of it is bunk?

The reason these things happen and the reason we can't get away from them is that we're created in the image of God, and therefore we have an awareness of a world and existence beyond the physical. It's hardwired into us; we naturally and instinctively believe in some sort of spirit world that transcends the physical world.

It has been said, "We are not physical beings with spiritual properties. We are spiritual beings with physical properties." Depending on the context, I can agree 100 percent. However, for our purposes we need to understand that we are equally physical and spiritual beings. If we separate the physical and the spiritual, we do so to our peril.

We can find freedom only when we operate within a unified physical and spiritual realm. There is a physical world we can see and there is a spiritual world we can sense, and they are one and the same. To try to operate in one world while ignoring the other is naive. Yet many influential people have encouraged us to operate just this way.

Plato and the ancient Greeks didn't deny there was an unseen spirit world. What they did deny was that the physical world had much importance. Plato said the only thing that matters is the spiritual and that everything we see in the physical has the same object existing in the spiritual realm, which is the real, true, and honorable object. What we see here is only a cheap facsimile of what's out there somewhere else in a truer form.

It was in Plato's worldview that the Roman Catholic belief of transubstantiation had its genesis. The medieval church (heavily influenced by the Platonic philosophy) melded Jesus' literal words—"this is my body and my blood"—with Plato's spirit world concept and began to teach that there is a meta-morphosis of the bread and wine into Jesus' literal body and blood. They believed this could happen because the physical world is only a shadow and reenactment of what's really happening in the spirit world. It is in the spirit world where Jesus exclusively resides, or so they believed.[2]

Another example of believers in the anti-physical world is the stoics. They practiced disassociating from physical pleasure since they thought only the spiritual should give us pleasure. This also fits hand-in-glove with deviant forms of religiosity in which the "devout" person literally beats himself up—sometimes as a form of penance and punishment, sometimes just to prove that flesh and physical matter have no significance or power. I don't know if self-mutilation sounds like freedom to you, but it definitely doesn't to me.

On the extreme opposite side from the stoics are those who deny the existence of a spirit world. Obvious examples are intelligent and well-known atheists in history and the present. Their ranks include Voltaire, Carl Sagan, Richard Dawkins, and Sam Harris. But by and large, humanity has always believed in the spiritual, even though we rarely agree on the finer details or the cohesive system that governs and explains it. Because all humans are created in the image of God, total disbelief in the spiritual will never move beyond a minority position.[3]

---

2. I'm not cracking on or attempting to discredit Catholicism. I believe transubstantiation is wrong, but I also believe that every belief system has things in it that are wrong. This includes my belief system, because I'm sure it contains inaccuracies—though I don't know what those are yet. Otherwise, I'd be changing them.
3. Genesis 1:27.

What puzzles me most is the number of professing Christians who are skeptical of the spirit world. Some will deny it. Some will give it lip service. Few will incorporate its awareness and the ensuing appropriate actions into their day-to-day lives. But if you actually read the Bible, you have to acknowledge the presence of the spirit world and realize how deeply it affects us. Some people are so afraid of what they don't understand that they'll rationalize anything. Despite Jesus and the early church encountering demons, seemingly in the normal course of their day, many of us pooh-pooh that sort of thing as ridiculous for educated people living in the twenty-first century.

If that's what we believe, can we really claim to be educated? No culture that has ever existed has failed to embrace a spiritual world filled with things that can't be explained by the physical sciences. The cultures rarely agree on their interpretations of the spiritual, but they agree there *is* a spiritual. Consider the ancient Greeks, Incans, Mayans, American Indians, African witch doctors, sorcery, Kabala, and a whole host of other religions and groups of people that would sacrifice children or virgins in order to appease the spirits. So why does every culture in the history of civilization have spiritual beliefs? Can there be any rational and educated conclusion other than that all humans believe and are tapped into the spiritual because the spiritual exists?

As a reader of the Bible and as a believer in the God of the Bible, I can't get away from believing in a pervasive spiritual realm that is constantly invading and influencing the physical realm. I also have a huge problem with saying, "I follow

Jesus, believe in His life and teachings, and want to model my life after Him, but I fundamentally disagree with the nature of the world as He described it." What is that?! Believing in Jesus means not only that I'm into charity and forgiveness, but that I believe Him when He talks about the realm I can't see by myself. And according to Jesus, that spiritual realm has innumerable evil personalities who are actively at work. What are they at work to do? To put you and me in bondage. To pull the rug out from under our freedom.

The person in charge of these evil personalities is Lucifer (a.k.a. Satan, the adversary, the deceiver, the devil, and a few other monikers). He isn't just trying to make you poor or physically disabled. He's going for the brass ring: he's trying to take you captive. He is trying to divide and conquer: to divide you from God and to conquer you so that you're in a prison where you have no mobility and are unable to have a satisfying relationship with God. He can use poverty or physical disablement to distract you from God and make you bitter, which is bondage. But he can also use prosperity and health to put us in bondage, because the more we have and the more problem-free our lives become, the less we think we need God. Yes, he is a cunning and conniving carnivore.

When something is going wrong in this world, it's a sign that the world is a broken place and in need of the freeing power of God. We inhabit a battlefield where spiritual forces are fighting, toxic things are happening, and spiritual beings are afflicting some of us in unique ways.

I have a friend who has plenty of money according to nearly any standard in the world. He has a company car. He has some savings for his kids' college years. He lives in a three-thousand-square-foot house and earns six figures. For the purposes of this book, I'll call my friend "Steve" (even though his real name is Bill). Steve is continually haunted by the fear that he won't have enough money in the future. This fear weighs on him like a wet sweatshirt.

He has regular breakthroughs only to lose ground again. Days of gratitude for all that God has done for him will be followed by days of fear about his 401(k). His moments of joy in worship services are overshadowed by driving home and wondering how he is going to afford his next car. Pride and joy in his great kids periodically give way to his angst about them expecting an Ivy League college education he can't afford.

What Steve knows is that this ever-present paranoid condition is largely inherited because he is the son of first-generation immigrants from Germany. His parents landed at Ellis Island not knowing anyone in America and not being able to speak any English. Their great work ethic enabled them to learn English, build a life, and launch Steve into a corporate career with high earning potential. I believe the combined situations of his parents' assimilating into American culture and their launching Steve into a successful American dream life not only afforded him many blessings but also created the potential for a stronghold. It may be not just a family pattern but instead an actual demonic personality that is afflicting Steve with doubts and concerns, which are robbing him of emotional freedom.

I'm hoping that you can see that when a person has a stronghold—some kind of lie they believe—that belief changes who they are. They agree to it, consciously or not, and it becomes part of them. At that stage in the game they either have bought into a normal system of the fallen world or have an evil personality residing inside them (possession) or afflicting them externally (oppression). That's the point at which they have bought into the evil system, are no longer asking questions, and are, at least in that part of their heart, owned by the spiritual forces of darkness. Sounds like sci-fi maybe, but it's reality. Jesus dealt with demons a *lot*, and they didn't just go away into some cosmic deep freeze when He left the earth.

When Jesus encountered a problem, He always engaged it as if something was wrong and needed to change. In other words, He never acted in a way that said, "God has a reason for everything, and He is either causing this pain or allowing this pain to happen to you. Therefore, look for the silver lining and see how it will make sense in the future." No. When a storm was causing harm, He spoke directly to it and commanded that it "be still." He rebuked it in a way that a person rebukes another person.[4]

Jesus once spoke directly to an evil personality who had overtaken a man and asked its name. Yeah, that's weird. When Jesus walked around, people who had demons would fall down and shriek.[5] He confronted multiple evil personalities in one person.[6] He also encountered people who had physical problems because a spirit was causing them; He healed them

4. Matthew 8:26; Mark 4:39; Luke 8:24.
5. Mark 3:11.
6. Mark 5:9.

by driving the evil out and encouraged His followers to do the same thing.[7] That alone is a pretty staggering thing. Have you ever considered, even once, that some of the physical problems occurring around you may be spiritual in nature at their root? Well, Jesus certainly acted as if that were true. And it wasn't okay with Him.

Jesus always treated everything that put people in bondage as being something against God's will. He never said or implied that God was content with anything evil in our world. He acknowledged the evil and the person and minions behind it. I love that Jesus was such a freedom fighter. That's exactly who I want to be, and when I think of Him defending people from bondage like that, it makes me want to do something outrageously brave and honorable with my life.

Jesus even encountered demons in people who were in the middle of serene religious services,[8] and yet some people who are in nice churches today—and profess to believe in the Bible and in Jesus—dismiss the possibility of an evil spirit bringing evil into their world, let alone into their church or personal lives. Could it be that certain things we struggle with continually and habitually are a result of a personal force coming against us? Why not?

The demonic realm, as it affects us personally, can be understood by comparing it to a germ. Think about it: germs are external entities that attack us and try to make us sick, which puts us in bondage—the bondage of lethargy or the bondage of a cough or the bondage of a hospital bed. Just as not all germs

7. Matthew 10:1.
8. Luke 4:33–36.

affect all people, not all demons affect all people. Just as germs come from the outside, demons come from the outside. And just as germs can be conquered, demons can be conquered. In fact, demons are always conquered when Jesus comes against them. And just as there was a day before the microscope existed that people doubted the existence of germs, people still doubt the existence of bondage-inducing demons.

While Jesus can and does heal us of physical and emotional trauma, whether from germs, personalities, or normal events, it typically doesn't happen overnight and sometimes doesn't happen at all during this life. Before writing this off as grossly unfair, let's go back to the beginning and remember that God gave us a world of freedom, and when humans abused that freedom, sin and all its negative effects rushed into this world. So we now have a world where things naturally go wrong even without the direct influence of an evil personality. Much of our growth and freedom will be a process that takes a long time—as was the case with the nation of Israel coming out of bondage. Unfortunately, there were individuals in the nation of Israel who never fully experienced all the upsides of freedom.

Some of us or our loved ones will have difficult physical or emotional problems that may not get resolved. That isn't because Jesus isn't real. It is because there are no simple answers, nor simple formulas in a world at war—there is more than meets the eye. First Corinthians 13:12 says, "Now we see but a poor reflection as in a mirror; then we shall see face to face. Now I know in part; then I shall know fully, even as I am fully known."

Nevertheless, strongholds that keep us in bondage can be broken. There are things you thought you could never get over, but you can. Some of you who are reading this book will experience freedom by simply telling whoever is afflicting you—whatever evil personality is there—to leave. Your freedom could be as simple as that. For most people, though, getting untangled from the web of lies is a lot like following Jesus: it's a major moment followed by a thousand small steps.

Maybe you've already identified something that's holding you back from experiencing real freedom, and you're ready to break the strongholds that are keeping you in bondage. If so, that's great. Keep reading.

Chapter 8

Evicting the Squatters

While strongholds can be established suddenly, they typically don't develop fully overnight. Imagine you wake up tomorrow morning, pour yourself a bowl of Colon Blow, and look out the back window past the deck and unused furniture to find . . . a tent. Just a two-man job, not very big, perched in your backyard. What do you do? You could go raise a ruckus, flex your muscles, and get it off your property, but you could also take a more laid-back, "civilized" approach. Maybe you think, *I don't know what that tent is doing there, but I certainly wasn't using my backyard last night, so whoever put it there is welcome to it. They're certainly not harming anything by being there.* So you leave them.

They're still there a week later, and you actually see smoke coming out of a little stovepipe in the top of the tent. *They've built a fire in there? How long are they planning on staying, anyway?* But being easygoing, you think, *Well, it* can *get a little chilly here at night. I might do the same if I were them.* And again, you leave them.

It's been six weeks now, and you come home from work to find a concrete slab poured under the tent (which has now been fortified with a wood frame) and a mailbox out front. Apparently these losers plan to stay for good. *Who do these people think they are?* By this time you are preoccupied with many other things in life, so you choose the path of least resistance as you convince yourself, "It's just a little concrete. No harm done." And you leave them be.

This goes on and on and on. Imagine that children are born in that tent, which expands to become a hut, then a shack, then an A-frame house. And those children grow up believing the property belongs to them, not you, and that they have every right to tear around your yard, crush the azaleas, and terrorize your dog. Imagine that they post a notice that squatter's rights came into effect after they were there for a few years, and now you couldn't oust them even if you tried. Are you starting to feel a little powerless, a little duped, and thinking that maybe you were too patient and understanding? Well, what if your children started to grow up thinking that those people belonged there and the property wasn't yours to begin with? Feeling any indignation yet?

You know, there's only one person to be blamed for these thieving vagrants staying longer than just that first night: *you*. You let them stay. You weren't a watchful owner. You thought it would be easier to avoid conflict than to be vigilant. So you ended up volunteering what was rightfully yours. But the truth is, you could still, at any point, run them off the property and tear down whatever they've built. You could uproot that concrete, plant new shrubs, and rehabilitate your traumatized acreage. You're the rightful owner; you have authority. Squatter's rights? Give me a break.

The exact same thing has happened to all of us, to some degree or another, in the spiritual realm. We have a real spiritual enemy who's come up alongside us with a little lie—like,

"Hey. You're worthless"—that may have been planted in childhood or in high school or in your job. You believed it, and when you did, you let it sit there. If you had God's truth or I.D. (in this case, that you're His child and nobody can take your place in His heart), you might have been able to combat it at the time—to throw that "squatter" off the lawn. But you didn't, so you were a victim. The lie spread out its tent posts and started expanding. Within a few years you believed that people don't love *you*; they love your money or your coarse humor, so maintaining those things is the only way to keep friends around (or a marriage together, or your children proud). Your choices started to be determined by this "I'm worthless" belief system, and now you have to have the latest trends in fashion (or technology, or car styles) because you don't believe you have inherent value in yourself. Before long you don't know who you are apart from this belief system. It lives on your property—and you might not even recognize it any longer. If you are starting to feel uncomfortable, that is a good thing. You could be realizing that someone has squatted and that hard work lies ahead. But be encouraged. That means a new state of freedom is right around the corner.

These insidious strongholds are bad news and definitely keep you from freedom. The gospel of Jesus Christ is good news. Not just good news that I'm going to heaven, but also the good news that right now God approves of me and accepts me. When I know and feel that approval from God, then I don't have to work for the approval of others. This is yet another way that Jesus has set me free . . . free indeed![1]

---

1. John 8:36.

The worst possible thing is your not even knowing they are there or choosing to believe they belong there. But if you've asked a few friends what they think of how you behave, or you've decided to open yourself up to what God wants to say to you, and you think you have a problem area identified, what do you do then? How do you walk up to those losers who you have just discovered have been mooching your stuff for years and years? It can be a frustrating, painful realization, and it's going to be uncomfortable to deal with something you've grown so accustomed to, but in the name of freedom, you've got to move those conniving personalities out, no matter what.

Just telling them to leave is a very real possibility. That's what Jesus did. He just said, "Come out," and they left the body. It's a matter of authority, and Jesus' authority trumps theirs all day long. If you're a Christ-follower, you have been given authority to deal with evil spirits[2] and can expect to do everything that Jesus did.[3] So you might have to say, out loud (and yes, you might feel nuts doing this, but get over it), "Anger (or self-pity, lust, bitterness, pride—whatever), I know you're there. You've been messing with my family and my work and almost everything I have been doing for the last twenty-five years. Well, I don't agree with you anymore, and I'm not allowing you to terrorize me another minute. *Leave!*"

The Bible teaches that the words that come out of our mouths are powerful. Think of how God made the world. He

2. Matthew 10:1.
3. John 14:12.

did it with His words. He spoke. The Bible says that both good words (that create life, hope, and love) and bad words (that create depression, confusion, and pain) have spiritual power and can help to create either strongholds for the enemy or towers for God in you.

My friend Steven Manuel was a major force in crafting this chapter. When he was in seventh grade, he was a chunky monkey. Even though he played football, he still was called a "fat ass" on more than one occasion by a small group of jocks who were shaving at age twelve. He eventually grew out of the "husky jeans" phase into the virile oak tree of a man he is today (he made me write that), but he never forgot those insults. Even when he was lean in later years, the scars of those words still impacted who he was.

In a similar vein, a number of years ago our church hired a consultant who was tainted by grossly inaccurate information. He said to me, "I can assure you with 100 percent certainty that any organization you lead will be hurtful and dysfunctional for those who work for you." Even though our staff now participates in national surveys that show they are off the charts in health and joy and we have been an award-winning organization multiple years running, that statement still haunts me. You can't say I'm crazy for letting those words affect me, because hurtful words from your past are still affecting you to this day. It's time we take a baseball bat to those lies.

Did you read or watch that scene in *The Two Towers* in the Lord of the Rings series, in which Gollum has an argument with himself in the forest about whether or not Frodo can be trusted? In this scene Gollum realizes for the first time that he can actually tell the bitter, accusing voice inside him—the one that's been plaguing him for years—to "go away . . . and never come back!" and he starts saying it over and over. He feels such empowerment from ousting the very spirit that has tormented him for most of his life that he starts dancing around. (Several people in the Bible did the same thing when Jesus freed them from the enemy.) That's a picture of freedom, and it's as simple as speaking to those personalities and telling them to get lost.

Even better than going through this alone, you can grab a person or two who support you in your faith journey and have them pray with you. The Bible says there's additional strength when somebody else is there to legitimize a decision we're making.[4]

When I'm helping people get through a stronghold in their past, I often look at it like a contract. When you agree with a lie, like you'll always be fat or your organization will always be dysfunctional, you're making a legal agreement that you will submit to the untruth. You say, "Okay, on this one, I'll sign over my rights. You got me. Come on in." And until you break it, the contract stands.

Right now you might be thinking, *But I never signed a contract!* While you probably never actually signed anything or agreed to any terms, your silence and compliance are all that is necessary for an agreement in the spiritual world. The same principle is reflected in the legal world in the law of "adverse possession," which provides eventual

4. Deuteronomy 19:15.

property rights for someone who lives on grounds they don't own for long enough. That's why legally savvy landlords evict squatters instead of allowing them to stick around. The alternative—to allow squatters to stay—means they'll end up forfeiting what's rightfully theirs.

Once you're finally sick and tired of being sick and tired and you're ready to kick those squatters to the curb, you can say—again, out loud, and having some people around is great—"This contract is no longer valid. I break this agreement with you, Fear (or whatever), and I know that I have the authority to do it because Jesus' blood invalidates this contract. Now #$@% off!" (You don't have to say the "#$@%" part, but it helps me.)

Two side notes about evicting the squatters before we move on: The first is that you have to understand that your enemy may have had a lifetime of success in this one area for you, and although he must leave when you tell him to go, he's not going to stay away. Strategically, it wouldn't make sense for him. He's got a proven winner in your stronghold; and your one moment of faith and courage, though it was effective, probably isn't going to keep him out for good. Jesus said in Luke 11 that the squatters *will* come back to the place they are used to residing. That can be intimidating, but only if you forget your authority.

You have to deal with the enemy and deal with him repeatedly. Now, keeping him off your lawn requires even more vigilance than evicting him in the first place. This is what the Bible calls temptation, and it happens over and over for all of us in the places where we're the most vulnerable.

I'm not tempted to murder, because that's not one of my weak spots. But lusting? Sure. The enemy's had a lot of success there in my past. Think he'll try that one again? Sure he will. So I have to stay on guard in that area. I don't want that stronghold to be built back up. The apostle Paul, who wrote most of the New Testament of the Bible, said that we shouldn't let the devil even get a toehold in our property,[5] because he'll always expand his territory if he gets in. That's how beachheads or strongholds are established.

Another friend of mine, Michael, who struggled with a cigarette addiction for years, always said he was great at quitting smoking: he did it two or three times every year! "The problem for me," he said, "was starting back up again. Quitting was the easy part." And keeping the squatters out of an old stronghold is a lot like quitting smoking—you might have to deal with temptation a hundred times on the day after you evict them. But by the second week, you're only dealing with them five times a day, and by the second month, you're not tempted much at all. You continue to be vigilant, but it's not a constant battle like it may have been at first. That's because you're getting stronger and he's getting tired of losing. That is freedom.

Finally, don't allow your property to just sit there when you kick the enemy out of it. Jesus says that the real danger is having previously inhabited territory unoccupied.[6] Don't just evict the squatters; start planting in that dead spot where they used to live. For a lot of people, that means creating new

5. Ephesians 4:27.
6. Luke 11:24–26.

habits that are free of those old strongholds. Let's say your stronghold is terrorizing nightmares, but you regularly go out on Friday nights with friends, looking for horror movies because they give you a little thrill. Start by telling the devil where to get off, and then start making some new habits. Buy season tickets to a local playhouse. Don't just sit at home concentrating on how you're not going to go see *Saw 666*. That's stupid. Create an alternative where horror movies don't figure into your life. Join a bowling league or something.

This is another great place to utilize people in your life who love you, know where you struggle, and want to help you get free. They'll keep you honest when you start to cover something up. If you say, "I think I've got that twenty-year alcohol problem under control. It's been three weeks already! Let's just go to Octoberfest—for the great music!" they'll be strong when you are weak or deluded. Friends who will volunteer as watchdogs for your old strongholds are the best friends in the world. Find them (or pray to find them if you don't have them) and use them.

The best thing to do, though, after you've identified a stronghold, gotten brave, and evicted the enemy, is to ask God to fill you with more of Him. Think about it: the devil has been camped out on your lot, stealing space that belongs to God. Both you and the devil have been pretty comfortable with that arrangement for years. It would be nice if there was some kind of holy security guard who could back you up, start planting fresh grass, and help get the place back in order, right? Well, God makes Himself available for just that service to us, and the only thing we have to do is invite Him onto the premises. Once you have evicted the squatters, it's time to experience the Holy Ghost—also known as the Holy Spirit. It's the Ghost who is going to give you the power you don't think you have and who has been filling your mind and heart with good stuff.

Chapter 9

Experience the Ghost

J ust once I'd love to have superhero powers on the basketball court. I'm a very average player who only hits the average mark because I hustle. I'm relatively slow, and I can't jump very high, but I don't wear down easily. Since perpetual competitiveness is one of my strongholds, I'm often wanting one more game; so the longer the game goes, the more effective I am.

People who play with me long enough eventually learn this and adjust their game accordingly. The guy guarding me knows I'm unlikely to juke left and drive around him for a layup, so he plays me really close, and it's hard to hit my jumper. But man, just once I would love to be able to juke right, drive left, and sky over the top of my man on the way to jamming the ball through the net. What I wouldn't give for superhero powers for just one day on the court. All I would need is one day, and that memory would keep everyone honest for years to come.

Over the past few years, superhero movies have been growing in popularity, featuring Superman, Batman, Ironman, the Hulk—the list goes on. The most popular movies connect with us on a deep level, and I believe that what moves us are the stories that tap into the truth of God. We love good guys wasting the bad guys, big adventure, and rescue. That's God's story. And because we're made in the image of God, we feel and want things that God feels and wants.[1] We're wired for rescue because rescuing is in God's character. Many of us are deeply moved by father–son stories because God designed fathers to have awesome relationships with their sons, which parallel our relationship with Him.

I guarantee I'm not the only one who wants to be like the Hulk. Believe it or not, you actually *can* have superhero-like powers. Jesus talked about this before He left earth. In His last monologue to His close friends before He was killed criminal-style on the cross, He said, "I'm going to ask the Father to send you a Counselor who will be with you forever—the Spirit of Truth. Others outside of a relationship with Me won't accept that Spirit because they are unaware of that presence's possibility. You won't be left as an orphan."[2] Jesus calls it out plain as day: He gives us power directly from Himself.

The Holy Spirit is about equipping you to do things you can't do naturally. The Holy Spirit is about giving you power that others who don't know Jesus can't have. The Holy Spirit can enable you to do things right now that you think are impossible. Things like jamming a basketball? Okay, yeah, He could, but He's more likely to do things that will give you true freedom.

It's possible that you have been burned by people who talk about the Holy Spirit a lot. But please don't let a few bad experiences or unhealthy people keep you from exploring a unique power that can change your life in the here and now.

1. Genesis 1:26.
2. John 14:16–18, paraphrase.

I had plenty of reasons to not seek the power of the Holy Spirit. Shortly after I decided to follow Jesus, I was feeling on top of the world—that is, until a group of friends told me I wasn't getting "all of God." They talked about a "second touch of the Holy Spirit." This didn't make sense to me, because I thought I had definitely sensed and received the Holy Spirit when I received Jesus.

According to those friends and the sound-bite scriptures they pointed me to, apparently something was missing. They asked if I ever spoke in languages I never learned. Other than burping, my answer was no. According to them, if I didn't speak a "prayer language" or "in tongues" it was evidence that the Holy Spirit wasn't fully present in my life. They said that all I needed to do was ask for the "filling of the Holy Spirit," and they would lay hands on me and pray. Then a whole new level of spirituality would be mine for the taking.

We sat down to pray, and I asked for the Holy Spirit, and the guys around me prayed for me, and then . . . nothing. They asked, "Do you feel it? Can you speak in tongues?"

"I don't know. Nothing is spontaneously coming out of my mouth."

"Well just try."

Nothing.

"Just start saying stuff," they said.

"What stuff?"

"Any stuff. Just let yourself go and allow the Holy Spirit to take over."

I was so confused. So they told me I should just start saying anything in a gibberish way. This would "prime" or jump-start my tongue into moving effortlessly and spiritually. But nada. Nothing. So this is what I mean when I say Christians (even well-intentioned ones) can point you into a life of religious bondage instead of freedom. Where I was joyful in my relationship with Jesus, now I was troubled. And when you're fresh in the life of following Jesus, other Christians' well-intentioned advice can be confusing. Sometimes instead of going straight to the source (the Bible), we get our pointers from others who might not have the best or fullest answers.

In a way, I was unintentionally spiritually abused and it kept me from being free as it related to things of the spirit world. But if every time "tongues" or something related to the Holy Spirit comes up and I instinctively flinch and become pessimistic and defensive, then I'm also not free.

Don't be afraid of people who seem a bit strange. In fact, don't even be afraid of what they are teaching. I would still love to speak in a language I've never formally learned. You can't allow a fear of the strange to keep you from obtaining the superhero-like powers God wants to give you. Trust me: *You need whatever power God will give* to be fully free in the most powerful way. You need to be aware of the spirit world.

*

The Bible isn't a mathematical or scientific journal that will help you exhaustively measure and understand everything in the physical realm. The Bible is a true story of God interacting with people. If you begin reading and understanding the Bible, you will find case after case of the supernatural. You will see regular, physical people coming in contact with the spirit world. You'll also see God manifesting extraordinary power through His Holy Spirit.

God exists as God the Father, Son, and Holy Spirit/Ghost— the Trinity. God as one and yet three beings at the same time is a heady concept that a sound bite can't explain; nor could a chapter, and maybe not even an entire book. But what you can understand, at least to the degree that they can impact your life, are the workings of the Holy Ghost and the reality of the spirit world. Understanding these things will lead you to deeper experiences of freedom.

Most people today refer to this spirit as the Holy Spirit, but up until the mid-twentieth century, most referred to Him as the Holy Ghost. These days I like referring to Him as "Ghost," because when we think of a ghost, we think of a personal entity, a person instead of an aura. Pop spirituality is all about auras (i.e., "May the force be with you"). An aura is a vague thing—not like a person who can inhabit you, empower you, and do amazing things.

Earlier we looked at the beginning of Jesus' monologue in John 14. A couple of chapters later He is still instructing and says, "If you love me you will obey what I command. And I will ask the Father, and he will give you another Counselor to be with you forever—the Spirit of truth. The world cannot accept him, because it neither sees him nor knows him. But you know him, for he lives with you and will be in you."[3]

3. John 14:15–18.

Jesus the Son is talking about the Father, who will send the Ghost. He says, "Guys, I am going to send you somebody who is going to counsel you since I can't always hang around. This counselor is going to be a personal spirit entity."

It is critical that you understand that the Holy Spirit is a person, not an "it." He isn't a force, though He can be forceful. He isn't a movement, though He will move you. He isn't a sensation, though sensations sometimes come when He is around. He isn't a principle, though principles He purports are always true.

The first time my wife, Libby, saw me was from twenty feet away while looking at the back of my head. She leaned over to her mother and said, "I'm going to marry that guy." Later on she talked to her brother and friends and told them she had met her husband. This all happened long before she ever actually met me.

I assure you that Lib isn't a wack job. She doesn't go around indiscriminately saying, "God told me." In fact, I can't remember a single other time she has ever said to me, "God said so." That's a good thing, because husbands generally don't respond very well to that line of reasoning. At least not husbands like me. "Honey, God told me that you are to cook me quiche every morning." Um, I don't think so.

Yet this time she told people that God said we were going to get married. She didn't hear an audible voice, but she did "hear" some internal counsel. That internal counsel was the voice of the Ghost. The Bible teaches that when you are adopted and enlisted into the Kingdom, God implants His Spirit in you. Literally.

*

Jesus told His followers He was sending a "Counselor." He wasn't sending a philosophy. He wasn't sending an ideology—not even a spirituality. So, He sends—directly to you—a personal Counselor. A counselor is a person who knows you and gives unique insight for your advancement. How cool is that?

Current pop spirituality operates like a mist or odor. It goes away. On the other hand, God's Ghost doesn't evaporate. God doesn't go away. He will never leave. Never. And He isn't a counselor who needs to be paid half your mortgage before He gives His services.

The revolution of freedom that's happening in you is the direct work of the Spirit who inhabits you and is counseling you. If right now you're beginning to feel and understand new things about freedom, there's a reason: the Holy Ghost.

A few months ago I ran into a guy I know named Wayne. I said, "How are you doing?" He said, "I'm doing good." I noticed he was tan, and I said, "You look good. You're looking *really* good." It wasn't just his tan that made him look good, but also his countenance, his whole demeanor, exuded health and joy. And maybe I thought he looked extra good because the last time I spent significant time with him he looked extra crappy.

About two years earlier I sat in his living room trying to console and counsel him and his ex-wife. The night before, they had lost their daughter to a car accident. A drunk driver killed her. You just aren't supposed to outlive and bury your own kid. It is one of the systems in this world that's broken. When God fully has His way in this world, there won't be children dying from drunk-driving accidents.

I'd seen Wayne in passing, but I hadn't really talked with him at length until that day a few months ago. He said, "Yeah . . . God is really . . . He has really been healing me." Now, I ask you: what doctor or therapist out there could ever *possibly* heal someone of the pain and brokenness resulting from the loss of a child in a car accident? Are there any who could ever make such a claim? But God the Ghost had pulled up very, very close to Wayne and somehow, in a deep spiritual way, begun to mend his broken heart. As I walked away from Wayne, I said to myself, "*That* is what the Spirit does." The Spirit counsels and empowers in ways that startle the human mind. Wayne has recovered joy and purpose in His life because of God's power, which came through the direct agent of the Holy Spirit. Nothing else can do what God has done. That is a power that makes me want to shut my mouth and take off my shoes. That is the power of the Ghost Counselor. There's nothing wrong with professional counseling, of course. I've been there before, and I'm sure I'll go again. It's just that the empowering internal counsel of the Ghost can do things that an external counselor just can't do.

The Ghost gives you power and abilities that you didn't think you had. He gives you insights you didn't think you could gain. He gives you feelings you thought you could never recapture.

After Jesus established that the Ghost was a personal counselor, He went on to say, "I tell you the truth: It is for your good that I am going away. Unless I go away, the Counselor will not come to you; but if I go, I will send him to you."[4]

Jesus' friends were thinking, *This is not a good thing. You're the greatest motivational speaker we've ever heard. You do incredibly powerful things like physically healing people. You conquer demons and put religious people in their place.* But what Jesus was saying was that His presence and power were limited by time and space while He was in human form. Jesus couldn't physically be in two places at the same time. He couldn't always be with both His friend Peter and His friend John. But if He left, the Holy Ghost could come upon and dwell inside each of them and never leave them. That's why I would rather have the Ghost *in* me than Jesus *with* me.

You may think that if Jesus were physically with you it would be easier to believe in Him. It's hard to deny the existence of flesh and blood. But there isn't any evidence from the Bible to support the idea that it would be easier if we had lived during Jesus' time. In fact, the evidence found in the Bible shows us that people who witnessed a physical manifestation of God lost their faith very frequently. The Old Testament shows again and again how God's people see miracles but the next day rebel.

Think about one of Jesus' most committed disciples: Peter. When Jesus tells Peter that within twenty-four hours Peter will deny that he even knows Jesus, Peter doesn't believe it. He's experiencing a momentary buzz from being around Jesus. But as Jesus is arrested that night and is no longer by

4. John 16:7.

Peter's side, Peter doesn't have the internal power to count himself as a friend of Jesus. Three times he denies Him. And just hours before, he had sworn he would never leave Him.

This same guy, Peter, goes on to do unbelievably bold and powerful things in the years after Jesus is physically gone. How? Because what Jesus said would happen did happen. The Spirit literally settled into people who had given their lives to Christ, so they had a power that transcended normal human experience. How else could you explain an emotionally unstable flake like Peter transforming into one of the main leaders of the early church?

If you have decided to follow Jesus and have a relationship with Him, then you, too, have the Ghost in you. You have the same power Peter had. You have everything you need to be one of the spiritual greats that people will talk about for generations to come. You have power now beyond your normal physical abilities.

Recently my friends and I went to work on a woman's house. Her husband had died of cancer, and her house was falling apart. She just didn't have the physical or emotional energy to do basic home maintenance. As we were doing various projects like replacing the plumbing fixtures in her bathroom, I noticed she was uncomfortable receiving the help. While I was outside cutting a piece of wood, I again noticed the embarrassed look on her face. Impulsively I said, "Hey, thanks so much for letting us serve you today. It's really an honor. Thank you." I saw a look of relief spread across her face.

In that moment I realized that my prideful self doesn't like to freely receive. I would much rather work for something.

She was probably feeling the same way. So I just tried to put myself in her shoes; I think if someone said that to me it would make it easier for me to receive.

Anyone who knows me really well, especially someone who knew me twenty or twenty-five years ago, is probably thinking, *Brian Tome did what? He said what? Wait a minute . . . Brian Tome considered somebody else's feelings?* You see, the natural Brian Tome doesn't empathize. He can't put himself in someone else's emotional world. The natural Brian Tome is driven. He is purposeful. He has high resiliency but low empathy. He doesn't just all of a sudden, out of nowhere, have a sense of empathy for somebody and the right words to go with it. But the Brian Tome who is inhabited by the Spirit has empathy powers that transcend his normal self.

I am growing in empathy and in many other areas. This is being fueled by the personal counsel of the powerful Holy Spirit. If you have received Jesus, you are growing, too, through the power of the Holy Spirit—in ways you can't even imagine. That is what the Spirit does. "Where the Spirit of the Lord is, there is freedom."[5] God is transforming you into someone who is powerfully free in a way that people without Him will never experience.

*

For a lot of people, "hearing the voice of God" is a complete riddle: the concept is shrouded in mystery and incomprehen-

5. 2 Corinthians 3:17.

sible jargon. Some people talk about "impressions" from God; others say they "discern" something; and those of us with more earth-bound antennae are just standing by, waiting for the magic God-lightning to strike us too. But hearing God's voice is something that every single Christ-follower is capable of experiencing. Jesus said that anyone who belongs to God hears what God says.[6] So if every one of us can hear what God says, why aren't we more confident about it? Or why don't all of us hear regularly from God?

For starters, the over-spiritualization of hearing God's voice has hurt a lot of us. We think we're not quite up to the challenge of walking on the water, so maybe we should just be satisfied with going to church services, reading the Bible once in a while, and trying to be nice. Jesus died and rose again so that we could have a relationship with God. It is a back-and-forth kind of thing, and it involves communication from God. "But," we protest, "I'm not one of those super-spiritual people. God could never get through to a simpleton like me!"

You overestimate your power to thwart God. It has been said, "God's ability to speak is greater than your inability to hear." I love that. That means He can speak to a baboon if He wants to. (I mean, just look at the Bible: God successfully communicated to and through Balaam's donkey, the ravens that fed Elijah, the fish that swallowed Jonah—and you think He can't reach *you*?) I know we don't have heaven-splitting revelations every day, but maybe God is talking to you in places where you just don't attribute it to Him. Do

6. John 8:47.

you ever speak or act because your conscience is moving you? Then assume that it is the Ghost in you, moving you to make wise decisions. Or when you get good counsel from parents, friends, your accountant, or whomever, remember that "every desirable and beneficial gift comes out of heaven."[7] In other words, they were the vehicle through whom God provided you advice. Or haven't you ever had a fortuitous phone call, seen a beautiful sunrise, caught all green lights on the way to the hospital, or been hugged by your mom? If any of these even remotely apply to you, I'm going to say that those were moments when the Ghost was speaking. Are you listening?

If you're just starting to try to hear God's voice and want to exercise the faith to see that it's really Him, let me give you a tip: if a thought comes into your mind that's good, builds people up, and doesn't violate any biblical laws, reasonable social norms, or international tax codes, assume that it is from God and do it. Personally, I just assume those thoughts are from the Ghost, and I use my freedom and move on them. Be decisive.

You have to take a risk at some point if you're ever going to learn to live by faith. (Remember, down with fear.) After all, it is called "faith"—not "being totally certain all the time no matter what." That means there is an element of uncertainty involved. God is not trying to make this exercise as inscrutable as possible, but we do have to step out there sometimes on nothing more than a hunch.

7. James 1:17 MSG.

The Ghost, being a person, has a personality just like we do. Maybe yours is the Myers-Briggs ENTJ or INFP or something like that. You have likes and dislikes. I like mint chocolate chip ice cream. I hate double chocolate chip. You can't talk me out of those preferences; it's just the way I am.

The Ghost is the same way: he has likes and dislikes. He is a person who can get bummed out. He gets grieved.[8] He gets distressed. He is like a dove, and He can flee. *He can flee.* The Ghost is a sensitive being, and based on how you live your life, you will receive more power or lose what power you have. This doesn't mean that God isn't in you or God isn't upon you. When God commits Himself to you, it's over. You're in. And His Spirit in you will never leave. But the Holy Spirit does kind of hunker down when He's comfortable or flee a situation when He's not. It makes sense that we may not get His full power in those situations. When you are grieved, do people get your best?

As with an actual dove, noise can cause the Ghost to flee. "Noise" in our lives looks like disobedience, such as when we're tearing other people down. That stuff grieves the Ghost. But just as you can grieve Him, there are things you can do to encourage Him to be extremely present and thus work more power through your life. That means doing things like forgiving people, serving others, and building people up. We should "get rid of all bitterness, rage and anger, brawling and slander,

8. Ephesians 4:30.

along with every form of malice. Be kind and compassion-
ate to one another, forgiving each other, just as in Christ God
forgave you."[9] And there you have the kind of obedience that
He can smell a mile away. He digs it, and He hunkers down.
That's where I want to live.

I hope you *can't* sympathize with me on this one: I have
people who intentionally work evil against me. People who
tell lies about me. And when I find out, I could get angry—set
out to get them back and "serve them right." But if I did that, I
would lose. I would lose the sense of His presence. But if I pray
for my enemies—if I love them and forgive them—the Spirit
is encouraged.

Now, some of you are saying, "Oh, yeah, but what if . . .
[insert your excuse]?" But if you have that kind of attitude,
you have just grieved the Ghost and are missing out on the
full experience of Him. I'm not trying to judge; I'm just telling you that's the way it works. Think about it. If someone
encourages you and lives a life that's encouraging, you naturally want more of that person. You want to hang out with
that person. I think that's how the Ghost feels.

God isn't as complicated as we sometimes make Him
out to be. I don't understand everything about the Spirit; but
when I see Him, I know Him. When I sense Him, I know Him.
And I want more of Him. I want to know more of His power
and have more of His power.

A few months ago, I was doing bodywork on a newly
purchased but extremely used car, and I bought some of that

9. Ephesians 4:31–32.

rubber truck bed liner that covers all the rust and ugliness (awesome product). The directions said, "Always wear rubber gloves." I said, "I'm not wearing no stinking girlie gloves," so I did the project barehanded and suffered days of not being able to get the stain off. Days of showers, WD-40, special Auto Zone hand cleaner—no help. (Kerosene was the final answer, by the way.)

But having that truck bed liner stain on my hands was like the presence of the Holy Ghost. You can't rub Him off. When Jesus breathes the Ghost into us—when we make the decision to follow Him—we get marked, and that's permanent. So even though we can grieve Him, we can't shake Him off.

You are marked by the Freedom Giver.

After Jesus' life on earth was done and He'd returned to heaven, His friends and followers didn't focus on wearing crosses and getting involved in the amazing Christian retail market that was sure to spring up in shopping meccas like Capernaum and Lystra. No, these people were savvy enough to know that the big deal, once Jesus was gone, was the Ghost that He promised. That was where it was *at*. That was the power. Right before He left, Jesus blew His breath of the Ghost onto them to help cement it into their brains. As soon as He breathed, they felt the Ghost. That same Ghost of power is available to you, because when Jesus is in you, the Ghost is in you.[10]

Again, Jesus wasn't about creating religious artifacts or starting a moralist movement or becoming the center of an argument. He didn't have a political agenda. He came to save

---

10. Romans 8:9–11.

and give freedom, and He left the power of His Ghost as His final legacy-defining act. The same Ghost who pulled Jesus out of the grave is the Ghost who will pull you out of depression or addiction. He's the same Ghost who will provide supernatural comfort when you're going through a second divorce. He's the same Ghost who does miraculous healings and whispers thoughts to you. I want you to believe in His power, and I want you looking for Him and listening for His words in you. I want you to obey Him because He's trying to lead you into *life* and *power*. I want you asking for Him to be in you and around you and to fill you up all the time. If you're a Jesus follower, He is there, right now, in you. He knows how to speak in a way that you can hear, and He is waiting for you to make room for His movement in your life.

Like the truck bed liner stains on my hands, the Ghost marks you. You are set aside. But at the same time, you get to make choices. By how you live, you can make the Spirit pull back or you can enjoy the fullness and freedom of His power.

Chapter 10

Blahs, Break, Blues, and Blessings

t would be really nice to eliminate everything that is holding us back by simply grabbing hold of freedom and expecting a huge and immediate change. But as we've seen, it's rarely that easy.

Getting free relies on God's power, but it also almost always requires some work and persistence on our part. Believing that breaking strongholds and attaining freedom will be a piece of cake will deeply frustrate you and potentially make you want to give up once you've started the good work. So we have to be real about this. Like wars that last years and have complexities that sometimes escape the public eye, the fight for our internal freedom takes time as well. While Jesus has declared us free and made us free in the heavens, translating that to the physical reality of now—of today—will take hard work, time, and endurance.

Even though we will all go through unique cycles (and maybe in different orders), there are four general phases almost everyone experiences on the road to freedom: the Blahs, the Breaks, the Blues, and the Blessings.

The Blahs

If you've read the book of Exodus in the Bible, seen DreamWorks's *The Prince of Egypt*, or admired Charlton Heston in *The Ten Commandments*, then you know God gave Moses a vision to lead the Egyptian slaves—the Israelites—out from under the bondage of their slave masters and into freedom. The strange thing about the story is that these people weren't really thinking too much about freedom. God had to give the vision to Moses, who then had to cast that vision within the nation of Israel. They were lulled into satisfaction in their current situation—slavery—because they had been under Pharaoh's rule for generations. They couldn't see clearly; their bondage was deeply rooted.

As Moses responded to God and began negotiating with Pharaoh for the Israelites' rightful freedom, Pharaoh got annoyed. He began making life more difficult for the Israelites (as if slavery wasn't horrible and oppressive enough). This, of course, caused the slaves even greater dismay, and Moses got antsy and questioned the need to change the slaves' situation. He said to God, "Why have you brought trouble upon this people? Is this why you sent me?"[1]

Basically Moses was saying, "God, before You asked me to intercede and lead this nation out of slavery, things were okay. Predictable. Slavery isn't a barrel of laughs, but at least there wasn't the turmoil that I sense is about to happen."

This is the way many of us are. Life isn't all fun and games, but things are okay—predictable, known. No major tragedies. No ulcers. No big tension. But at the same time, there is no growth and no advancement. No purposefulness, no vision, no intimacy with God. Many people never break out of this

1. Exodus 5:22.

phase because they don't dream or expect that there could be other ways to live. They don't know any better and are either complacent or strangely content. Like the Israelites, they are in the Blahs.

Let me explain what it may look like when you're in the Blahs: you might barely have enough money to make ends meet. Maybe you borrow from Visa to Visa. (The average household's credit card balance is about twelve thousand dollars these days.) You aren't sure how your way of life can continue, but for the present month things are okay. Or maybe you have plenty of cash and all the toys money can buy, but you're bored out of your skull.

Maybe you're dating someone, and the relationship isn't bad, but it's not great. Somewhere along the line, sex began to be part of your relationship. Maybe the first time you had sex you second-guessed what you were doing, but now you're used to it. At the same time, sex is complicating things and making it that much more difficult for you to break up, but you probably don't recognize it as a complicating factor (which is one of the many reasons God counsels us to reserve sex for marriage). You aren't sure what to do, but you are within the realm of the predictable, and it doesn't seem worth the emotional toll, the arguments, the potential loss involved with making a change. You are in the Blahs.

Your kids might be blahs. I don't encourage you to tell them that to their faces, but you may just be enduring the child-rearing years instead of leveraging and enjoying them. Who can blame you? The demands of life are difficult. You may not realize it, but if you're not thriving, neither are your kids. (And you might not realize that they really annoy other people.) If you're in the Blahs with your kids, you're not in a satisfied relationship. You let things slide because you don't want to disrupt the "peace"—which might not actually be peace at all.

Sometimes the Blahs become the Brutals: when you can't deny that something is totally screwed up and you have no choice but to change. Usually before people get on the road to recovery, they realize they're on the road to addiction. Life isn't falling apart, but they sense that all the ingredients for falling apart are present, so they break from the Blahs and decide, "This is too risky. No more Jack Daniels." Or, "This relationship is just about lust. I'm finished." Others aren't so motivated. It takes a few failed relationships, eight jobs in four years, a bankruptcy, an intervention. But whether you're in the Blahs or the amped-up Brutals, there's something that needs to happen if you want freedom. It requires movement, though—not just talk, not just admittance.

Today I heard two adult men telling their stories. Andre is a twentysomething African-American who was recently hired for his first promising job. After making it through an impoverished and difficult inner-city upbringing, he enrolled in a mentoring program to help him find and retain a well-paying career. Now, if you purchased this book in a bookstore, you may have no idea why a young man would need to learn how to find and retain employment. "Just get a job" is the simplistic mantra of people who don't understand guys and girls like Andre. But when you have never had parental involvement and have lived in four different foster homes growing up, you miss out on learning basic life skills that some of us take for granted. Many of Andre's role models' only income was from the social service check they got for being a foster parent. Andre was never encouraged to learn and never watched a man develop a skill. He had never seen a man get up early and come home at the end of the day for five days a week. He never experienced a strong work ethic leading to a better job with more money and better benefits. He rarely saw anyone graduate. This entire scenario is an environment custom-made for enslavement to the Blahs; it keeps kids from being free.

When Andre decided he wanted to chart a different course in his life and sign up for a mentoring program, his friends criticized him. They asked him why he'd want to do that, and how and why anyone would help him. They told him he was wasting his time. Yet he realized that unless he learned new life skills, behaviors, and attitudes from someone else who was willing to work for his freedom, then nothing would ever change.

The freedom that Andre needed was going to require his breaking from the attitudes and mind-sets that still held his friends in bondage. He may even have to break from his friendships. To complicate things further, the freedom that Andre is going after is not going to pay rewarding wages for a while. That is exactly why many people in Andre's situation won't go forward to retain their freedom. Change is work.

It is a similar situation with my friend Jonathan, a forty-something white executive. He seeks to escape reality every night through one drink too many, and when things are really bad, through forty-five minutes of Internet fantasy porn. Those habits will continue until there is a break in his attitudes, assumptions, and prior programming. Even then it will be a while until the full effects of those habits drop away and he can experience the joy of being unencumbered.

Change—the movement—will be hard. You'd probably rather hide or deny what's going on because it seems easier. You'd rather wait around and just "see what happens." But that's giving up. That's not asking God to take you out of bondage.

The Break

America is an incredibly antagonistic society. We all want change in some way. We want the government to change or the Constitution to change. We sign petitions. We vote for people to make changes. We bemoan some of the changes that have already happened and hope that they'll change back, whether in regard to war, abortion, pornography, homosexuality, the national tax structure, gun control, or something else. The problem is, and I'll use Leo Tolstoy's words, "Everyone thinks of changing the world, but no one thinks of changing himself."

The Break is the moment you change—when you move out from where you are accustomed. It isn't the ultimate destination point. It's the first intentional step toward another place—a place of greater freedom.

Once I was speaking on this point of change and a guy came up to talk to me afterward. He was a little bummed at a comment I made about how we need to pass the tests and receive the freedom God is giving us, and when we don't, we don't grow. We keep a barrier between us and God. An example I'd given was knowing you have bitterness and unforgiveness toward someone and also knowing you need to release that bitterness. Well, the guy who approached me said, "It isn't that easy when you've been physically and sexually abused as a child for years. You can't just get over it."

I agree with that entirely. The Break won't be followed by a fifteen-minute true-or-false test. The Israelites suffered 430 years of the Blahs until one specific day when they broke. They took one big step of departure.[2] The process of breaking will usually require a long prep course from God and a series of changes to move completely out of the Blahs. Nevertheless, the Break itself is always a single moment in time, a defining point. The Break doesn't occur when everything is solved and simple. Instead, it is the moment when you turn your back on what has you in bondage and say, "I'm moving in a different direction." It's when you decide to let go because you want a healthier, more satisfying life without the dulling pain of relived memory. It's when you decide that consistent, seventy-hour workweeks aren't allowing you to build into your marriage and so you commit to and act upon a new schedule that honors your spouse. It's when you cut up your credit cards. It's when you decide that four drinks each night are numbing you to the full experience of life, so you quit drinking entirely. It's the moment you own up to the fact that

2. Exodus 12:40–41.

you can't go three months without being in a heavy dating relationship and so you take an intentional break and choose to fill your time, instead, with loving and receiving love from the people already around you. As Saul Alinsky, a radical backyard revolutionary of the 1930s, said, "Change means movement. Movement means friction."

The Break is not when you close this chapter and think, *Yeah, now I'm inspired.* That's only common sense. The Break is the first tangible act that is different and difficult. And you don't really know if the Break has happened unless it becomes common practice and the next decision you make follows the new direction.

For the Israelites, the Break was when they saddled up their camels and left Egypt.

When we try to make a break from previous patterns, all hell will break loose in trying to keep us where we are. Why am I telling you this? Because much of the physical world perfectly mirrors the spiritual world. When it comes to the DNA of change, the Break may be the most difficult step. We want to keep reproducing the same things we have always been and always done, just as a cell's DNA replicates the same pattern every time. If the cell suspects that the DNA is messed up, it will often self-destruct to protect the integrity—or status quo—of the cell. In the same way, when a new way of living is introduced, we are hardwired to think it is in our best interests to eliminate it and not change. We will defend to the death our picture of who we are and the role we think we fill prior to change.

Some of us are thinking, *That isn't me. I love change! I'm all about the new.* Could it be that change and the new are just expressions in your DNA of your inability to stick with any one thing for too long? Perhaps those closest to you might not say that you're into change but that the core of your nature is fickle and lacks follow-through and perseverance. Perhaps the change you need is less change in the externals and more change in your internal driving mechanisms.

When we are in the process of change, it doesn't always feel good. You'll have to take some new risks. You might be confronted with people who don't want you to change. If you aren't aware of this and prepared for it, you may regress or end up worse than you started. So it's really important to consider the friction beforehand so you're not derailed. Talking to God and relying on His Holy Spirit to empower you are critical during these times, and you'll want to pray throughout the day. Ask God for the specific strength you need and then receive what He gives you.

Having community with a trusted friend or two during the Break is also invaluable. You will need reassurance that you're taking the right step and people to keep you on track. The story about Andre is also a story about a friendship. Andre's trusted mentor and friend is an executive named Jim. Not only is Jim a male who represents hard work, but he is also a coach who gives Andre encouragement and physical empowerment. When Jim found out that Andre missed out on getting the last job he applied for because he couldn't drive a forklift, Jim pulled some strings and got him training that landed Andre the job. That's what having community looks like when you're in the midst of hard change.

And as you're making hard changes, be encouraged by what you'll eventually experience: "It is for freedom that Christ has set us free. Stand firm, then, and do not let yourselves be burdened again by a yoke of slavery."[3]

The Blues

Okay, the Blues. Here's the intermediate phase after you've made the break from old habits but haven't yet experienced the full blessings that eventually follow. The Blues are deceiving because they make you think what you used to have wasn't all that bad.

The Israelites' break was an amazing thing—just like your break might be a dramatic, energizing moment. After Moses led the Israelites away from their slave masters, Pharaoh changed his mind about granting them release and sent an entire army after them. This is when the barrier of seawater separating the Israelites' safety from their recapture was miraculously parted. The Israelites got to the other side (the pursuing army definitely didn't), and God was right there. They felt on top of the world. *But then* reality hit. They looked around and said, "Okay, now what?" They wailed, "I'm hungry. Where's the Taco Bell?" But there was no border-run in sight. No immediate food source. No immediate shelter. No immediate anything. They were starting from scratch, and scratch meant scarcity.

3. Galatians 5:1.

In the desert the whole community grumbled against Moses and Aaron. The Israelites said to them, "If only we had died by the LORD's hand in Egypt! There we sat around pots of meat and ate all the food we wanted, but you have brought us out into this desert to starve this entire assembly to death."[4]

If you can't identify with the Israelites, consider America's beginnings. America was a nice and comfy place until the first inhabitants decided to make a break from England. The defining breakpoint was the Declaration of Independence. But this break wasn't when the Blues came. That didn't happen until months later, because it took at least that long for the ships to get back to England to deliver the Declaration and then for England's war ships to come all the way back.

The Blues is no-man's land. No one wants to be there. In our old habits we have the comfort and security of the known. In our future promised land there await positive things yet to be experienced. But the area between those two places affords us only heartache and uncertainty. In transition, every change feels like failure. That's why most people go back to their old ways of enslavement instead of enduring through the difficult present to attain a preferred future.

The Blues often happen in marriage. I meet a lot of single people who think that as soon as marriage happens, immediate blessing will follow. But the Blues do come in marriage. For some, it's the seven-year itch. For Lib and me it came

4. Exodus 16:2–3.

earlier—after about seven hours. In fact, in our marriage we experienced a fifteen-year cycle of the Blahs until we finally realized that changes needed to be made, which meant breaking from previous habits. Then there was the waiting for those habits, disciplines, communication techniques, scheduling changes, and so on to kick in. That was the Blues stage—the time we had to persevere. (Finally the blessings came and we had a fresh, intimate, and exhilarating relationship.) For us, the Blahs, the Break, and the Blues were worth it.

A relationship in the Blues is almost never "fixed" by a quick counseling session tune-up. God must be involved. We need to recognize our limitations and the freedom He has designed for us. Throughout the whole process, we draw close to God—and that's what fires Him up: relationship. The goal is to lean into God and see what happens when His power couples with the tests you're passing. The goal isn't just the endpoint; it's what happens between you and God during all the hard work.

Some of us might have said in the past, "Hey, I'm not sure I want to get serious with God. I did that once and nothing happened." Maybe you decided to spend less time at work and more time with your family, but they haven't yet grown accustomed to your renewed presence. Maybe you gave up an addiction and you're feeling pissed off and empty. Well, you might be in the Blues and just have to endure it long enough to get to the next phase.

I began studying Nelson Mandela and South Africa when our church started to invest significant time and money into that region of the world. I found it interesting that Mandela was in prison for twenty-seven years, and then after he was freed his marriage lasted only three years. He can do twenty-seven years on a concrete block but only three years in a marriage? I say this not to be judgmental, but to remind those of us who are married that marriage can be hard. Really hard.

A friend of mine showed up on my doorstep about a year ago. He had confessed to his wife about having had multiple affairs. He felt awful about what he had done, but obviously not as awful as his wife felt. One of the things that she wanted assurance of was that, if she were to stay with him, it would never happen again. He told me that based on his past, he didn't know if he could promise her that. What if he actually let her down again? He had nothing in his history to suggest that he could change this.

I said to him, "You can commit to her. Tell her you'll never do it again." The difference in this situation versus others is that there were systems in place to help ensure that it wouldn't happen again. Not only did he now have the freeing power of the Spirit in his life, he had begun (or re-begun) a personal and intimate relationship with God through the power that Jesus offers. When you have that, it doesn't guarantee that everything is going to go fine, but it is an automatic system that includes things you do, experience, or receive on a regular basis that helps you endure. To get through the Blues it's necessary to anticipate this natural phase and counter it with some natural, automatic systems. The other system my friend had in place was regular weekly meetings with guys who would hold him accountable and encourage him. Since he made the decision to be automatically transparent—the

Break—he had an automatic system that could help him endure a painful blah in his marriage.

The key to changing and enduring through the Blues after the potential euphoria (or trauma) of the Break is to set up as many automatic systems as you can and never compromise them. For instance, the Bible's principles on finances and the decision to automate some of our finances are the sole things that enabled Lib and me to get into a solid financial place. Early in our marriage, we dreaded going to the mailbox, fearing the reminder envelope that represented another creditor we were in bondage to. Now that we are free, we view those biblical principles as unalterable, and when we learned to automate some of our finances—things like automatically depositing money into savings—things became easy and weren't bluesy anymore. We didn't stress about those car-insurance bills; we knew we had them covered.

The reason why we rarely change is that we don't like the things we have to *do* to change, and we don't want to endure the Blues that typically precede the good results. We all want to be financially secure, yet we might not want to give up certain extras. We all want good relationships, but we might not want to have automatic times set up to foster those relationships. We all want a deep relationship with God in some way, shape, or form, but we must set up automatic time with Him. Church isn't God, but attending a healthy church should be one of those automatic systems to help you have a relationship with God (just like Bible reading and prayer). You have to put the systems in place to support your break, and then you'll eventually find the outpouring of freedom you desire.

The Blessings

Here's how the story "ends" for the Israelites:

> So the LORD gave Israel all the land he had sworn to give
> their forefathers, and they took possession of it and settled
> there. The LORD gave them rest on every side, just as he
> had sworn to their forefathers. Not one of their enemies
> withstood them; the LORD handed all their enemies over to
> them. Not one of all the LORD's good promises to the house
> of Israel failed; every one was fulfilled.[5]

Both grace and justice bring great things into our lives.
Grace is when God's goodness and mercy overflow into our
life; it has absolutely nothing to do with who we are or what
we do. This is what Jesus implies when He says that God causes
the sun to rise on people who are both evil and good, and He
sends rain on both the righteous and the unrighteous.[6]

You will experience some level of grace regardless of how
you live your life. Even if you never change from who you
are today—with all of your quirks, selfishness, and sins—you
will still receive grace from God. But you will only be tapping
into 50 percent of the revenue stream, because the other ave-
nue for blessings is justice.

Justice can have a negative connotation, but in this case,
it's simply getting what you have put effort toward. If you've
stolen cars, you've worked toward jail time. If you and your

5. Joshua 21:43–45.
6. Matthew 5:45.

partner have worked daily for a good marriage, you will achieve intimacy.

Sometimes, blessings have downsides. The Israelites were blessed to be out of slavery, yet they articulated that at least while they were slaves in Egypt they had a place to be buried. Our blessings are never nirvanas. Most of the time they are just gateways to new tests, which are new opportunities for change, which are new opportunities for growth in our relationship with God.

The bottom line is that if you want the full experience of God's freedom, you have to be willing to put forth the effort to work through the hard times and persevere until you reach your reward. It's a full-on process that demands wholehearted devotion to change in one particular area at a time. A balanced, wait-and-see approach just won't cut it if you want to attain the blessings of the freedom God champions for us.

Chapter 11 —————

The Unbalanced Life

N ow that you're getting both a picture of the kind of freedom God offers us and an understanding of the phases that often accompany movement toward it, you might be ready to leave the Blahs behind and make a break of some kind. Maybe you have already changed some things and are feeling some major relief and renewed hope. That's awesome. You are tracking with what God planned.

Remember, though, what often happens when you're in the next phase of change: after you've made a break in your life and the rush is over, it might be tempting to give up and go back to your old ways. During the Blues, you might be tempted to pick up an old addiction and pass it off as just a temporary fix. You could go back to fighting for attention in the workplace by belittling others to get a group laugh. You could change your mind about asking your daughter for forgiveness because it just seems too hard and too embarrassing. You could shrug off your intimate relationship with Jesus by skipping prayer and Bible study because you have too much to do.

Or you can endure. You can evict the squatters and strongholds. You can claim the new identity you have in Jesus that is rightfully yours.

You can keep pushing toward freedom and the blessings that come from it.

The Israelites who were led into freedom continue to be a perfect example of how some people give up on freedom while others stick it out and receive benefits and blessings. Whether you've read the entire Old Testament or you're coming fresh out of the gates, you probably know the story of the Israelites crossing the Red Sea. Quick refresher: The Egyptians were holding the Israelites as slaves until Moses convinced Pharaoh to free them. Yet to finally get away from their captors, Moses (with God's power in him) split the Red Sea so the Israelites could cross to the other side and the pursuing Egyptians would be caught in the middle—that is, crushed by the deadly waves. Many people think that if they saw this kind of a miracle they would never have any doubts and enduring in God's principles would be easy. This wasn't the case with the Israelites, however, even though the miracle should have shown them that God was completely dedicated to their freedom and protection. I mean, an entire sea splits in half and the Israelites get a dry road to the other side? Of course, there's always a thick skull or two out there—and a moment that separates the boys from the men.

After finally escaping, Moses chose twelve leaders from the twelve Israelite tribes to do a scouting mission prior to moving into the land God had prepared for them and thus receiving all the blessings of their new freedom. These weren't just twelve guys who picked the short straw—these were the strongest of the strong, the ones with charisma, the ones with a track record. So Moses told them to go check out the property God set aside for them (a.k.a. the promised land) and return back with a full report. Remember, God had already told the

Israelites they would have to work for this land. It wasn't going to be served to them on a silver platter. But He also said He'd give them supernatural power (His) and go ahead of them to prepare the way. So the twelve leaders went to do the reconnaissance mission with their heads held high. But they came back with their tails between their legs.

"What was the promised land like?" the left-behind Israelites asked.

"Milk and honey. Gorgeous land, tasty food, fat goats . . . and a bunch of massive, grade-A country folk guarding the gates!"

I'm sure a hush fell over the crowd.

"There's no way we're getting that land. We can't do it," one of the leaders said. Then one after another after another nodded his head in agreement. They were giving up. But when it came to the eleventh scout, Caleb, along with the twelfth, Joshua, they said, "The land we passed through and explored is exceedingly good. If the LORD is pleased with us, he will lead us into that land, a land flowing with milk and honey, and will give it to us. Only do not rebel against the LORD. And do not be afraid of the people of the land, because we will swallow them up. Their protection is gone, but the LORD is with us. Do not be afraid of them."[1]

The answer to why ten people didn't go after freedom and attain its blessings when two did is tied to a deceitful maxim that existed in Israel's ancient culture and our modern culture as well: "live balanced." The perspective of the ten unfaithful

1. Numbers 14:7–9.

losers was one of levelheaded balance. "It's best to get your ducks in a row"; "Let's be reasonable"; "Let's not go out on a limb"; "Evenly divide yourself between God, family, work, church, friends," and so on. Most everybody seems to agree that this philosophy makes sense, but if you want to depress me, just tell me that I'm living a balanced life. Why would that bum me out? This time it has nothing to do with motorcycles and everything to do with wholehearted devotion.

If you're focused on maintaining balance—trying to satisfy all the people in every area of your life and just skating by with a little energy here and there—you probably aren't moving, and you probably aren't experiencing the blessings that come from a life lived in freedom. Striving for balance means you're not throwing your weight behind one focused effort because you're too spread out (and likely too exhausted) or have too much fear to make a commitment. But there are times in your life when you are going to have to throw your shoulder into something and push as hard as you can if you want to experience the fullness of God's blessings. This is what Caleb did—this forty-year-old Israelite.

The zero-to-forty age group is pretty notorious for wholehearted devotion. Teenagers throw their full weight behind getting the latest gaming device, achieving body beautiful, or getting the attention of the hottest guy in school. If you're thirty, you probably know what it feels like to go full-force into earning a promotion or buying a first home. Zero to forty is a natural period for this kind of passion, whether it's pointed at the right thing and driven by what we believe is going to please God and bring freedom or not. But the younger you are, the more likely you will be to go balls to the wall. (That's a piloting term, by the way. Seriously.)

At an age when most guys are starting to look for reasonable balance—forty—Caleb was saying that he absolutely wouldn't back down from the imbalanced dream of taking the promised land. At that time Moses said to him, "The land on which your feet have walked will be your inheritance and that of your children forever because you have followed the Lord my God wholeheartedly."[2] Then the Lord says this about the desert-versus-promised land scenario: "Because my servant Caleb has a different spirit and follows me wholeheartedly, I will bring him into the land he went to, and his descendants will inherit it."[3] He was free from balanced opinions and from wanting to please others.

Because Caleb had different fuel in his tank—a fire burning in his belly—he followed God full-on, and God decided to bless him remarkably through his life and his lineage. Caleb was living an unbalanced life for God. He wasn't fearful of making a commitment. He wasn't swayed into the "normalcy" of following others.

No one who has made a significant impact has ever had a perfectly balanced life. The book of Galatians gives some concrete guidelines to the idea of "living unbalanced." Even though Caleb lived long before Galatians was written, I think this principle defined his life: "Am I now trying to win human approval, or God's approval? Or am I trying to please people? If I were still trying to please people, I would not be a servant

2. Joshua 14:9.
3. Numbers 14:24.

of Christ."[4] The guy who wrote that was Paul—a man who started many churches in the New Testament era. In fact, he wrote most of the New Testament. And this guy could never be accused of being "balanced." He was super-passionate about living out the Kingdom by blessing other people and honoring God. Without Paul, who knows where Christians this day would be? Paul made it simple: please people or please God. Since he chose to please God, his life got way off balance.

When you're balanced, you don't bother anybody. You shrug your shoulders and avoid rocking the boat. But when you start getting off balance, you say, "This is where I'm going with my life." You start going places. You start leaving others behind because you stop trying to please only *them.*

It is really great when you please God and other people get pleased too. I love that. That's awesome. Everyone wins—especially you. But what Caleb does is stand in the minority, because ten of the other leaders were backpedaling and he was going forward.

When I first started going forward with Jesus, I was around fifteen or sixteen years old, and I had to stand in the minority. I had to throw my weight behind the decision to stop my underage drinking. This definitely didn't please my drinking buddies, but I said to myself, "I'm more concerned about pleasing God than pleasing these guys." I had to endure some difficult things that happened during those years, but I began making difficult decisions and accepting a minority stance. The crazy thing is that the guys I used to live my life

4. Galatians 1:10 TNIV.

for are people I don't even know anymore. I can't even remember the names of many of those friends I had thought were so important. Good thing I went wholeheartedly after God.

I also remember being a freshman in college and taking a psychology class with Dr. Heckle (no lie), who taught one day about how many believe that a belief in God could negatively affect the psyche. So he asked the class, "Does anybody in here profess to know God?" I started to get nervous. I looked around. I was going, *Okay, somebody's got to say something. Certainly someone else . . .* But no one said anything, and I could feel God pushing into me, as if He was saying, "Brian, you don't want to tell anybody that you know Me?" So I raised my hand, and then Dr. Heckle called me out. We had a little exchange that went okay, but what I remember is that it cemented the idea in my mind that I have to put myself out there. I don't want to be in that 90 percent, lukewarm, namby-pamby category.

Of course, sometimes you can be unbalanced and throw your weight into something and find out later that it wasn't the right direction. For example, I was coaching junior high football and felt that it was right to build winners and have the boys work hard. There was one kid, though, who always seemed to be last—always loafing. And he always seemed to be faking an injury. Well, at the end of the last year I coached, he came up to me on the sideline and he was crying. I asked him what was wrong, and he said, "Coach, I played two years for you, and I never got in for a single play." Thinking about that is difficult for me even today. I was wrong, and I really hurt that kid. I wish to this day that I could find out where he is and apologize. (John, if you're reading this, I am really sorry. I should have asked you to play.)

Sometimes wholehearted devotion doesn't go right. But to experience freedom we must feel free to throw our weight behind something—even if it might be the wrong thing. If it turns out to be wrong, we can circle back with a contrite heart and ask God for forgiveness. What I realize about that coaching experience is that I wasn't going after God; I was being wholeheartedly devoted to my image as a successful, tough coach.

But when your unbalanced and wholehearted efforts go right, it is beautiful. In my Cincinnati community we're backing an initiative to build and staff a huge facility to get people out of generational poverty. It's controversial in our city. Our church is supporting it—even though newspapers and picketers are speaking against it—because we want to please God more than we please others. We know that God is asking us to serve the poor, so it's balls to the wall.

On a smaller scale, when I talk about the environment during a church service, I can think, *Okay, so I have to have something in here for the Democrats and something for the Republicans and strike some sort of balance, right?* No, that's when things get wacked. That's useless, fake political correctness. Sometimes I'm going to say things like a flaming liberal, sometimes like a neo-radical conservative. My guideline isn't to balance the message for the masses but rather to throw my weight behind what I believe God is directing me to say. So when people come up to me after I speak and say, "You know, I really like this church except for ____ or ____," I say, "Hey, you have to understand: I'm not trying to please you. This is about God and trying to please Him."

This is how we obtain a beautiful and simple freedom: Instead of looking over your shoulder to figure out who needs what and how to keep Jim happy while you keep Chuck happy, or how to get away with not rocking the boat because you're worried about your image, keep focused on what will keep God happy. Period. If you mess up—and we all do, constantly—just dust yourself off and get focused again. God forgives.

Let's get back to Caleb, because his story didn't end at forty. After the ten other leaders gave up on the promised land, God said to them (in my paraphrase, just in case you aren't catching on), "You know, you people make Me sick. I brought you out of slavery. I parted the Red Sea. I do awesome things for you and you still don't believe Me. So here's the deal: Israel is not going to enter the promised land until you all die. I'm not going to come down and kill you. I'm just going to let you wander around in the desert until you're dead. You are going to have babies and bring up a new generation, and that new generation is going to go into the new land. But as for you, you're going to wander around the desert for forty years. When you're all dead, except for Caleb and Joshua, Israel can go on."

So Caleb had to live with the negativity and shallowness of the tribes of Israel until they all died off. He had to live from age forty into his eighties with wholehearted, enduring optimism. And it wasn't a walk in the park. I was in that kind of a wilderness a few years ago, and it's not the guidebooks' top pick for a number one vacation. It's hilly, rocky terrain with craggy things all over the place. The Israelites weren't walking around in well-supported Timberlands either. And they didn't have North Face tents and Nalgene water bottles. When you wander in the desert of the Middle East, most of your time is spent looking down at the ground to make sure you don't twist an ankle.

Even though we can walk in freedom, none of us is immune to periods in the desert. (You can find yourself in the Blahs at any point in life.) You could be in a desert as a result of your own free choices bringing natural consequences. If that's the case, God is trying to bring you to repentance. Turning away from a behavior could be the Break you need to escape the desert you're in.

Sometimes we are in the desert as a result of other people's choices, as was the case with Caleb and Joshua. If you are married and your spouse cheats on you, get ready to be in a desert. You probably aren't going to feel spiritually hydrated for a while. You are going to be filled with pain and doubts. In these times, throw your weight into learning all you can in the desert. God can teach you things there that you won't learn at a resort.

Finally, we will all go through periods in the desert for no apparent reason—no one makes a choice that lands us there. Following Jesus isn't a predictable mathematical equation that enables you to plug in the right values and right decisions to guarantee that everything will turn out okay. In fact, Jesus Himself wasn't immune to going through a desert period of forty days, so we should expect to do the same—maybe for forty days, maybe for forty years.

Caleb went through a desert simply because he was committed to God's promise. When everyone died off as God said they would, except for Caleb and Joshua, it was time to leave the dry and arid place to take over the promised land. That new generation, passionate and wholeheartedly devoted, was on board with Caleb and headed toward their inheritance.

Do you know how Caleb took it one step further? When they started dividing up the land—portioning out who got what pasture and watering hole—Caleb announced that he wanted the hill country. He wanted the best blessings—and the hardest stuff. Because if you remember playing king of the hill, you know that the most powerful person stays on top of the hill, but that person also has to work the hardest to keep it. The "king" has to push some kids into the gravel when they start attacking. And that's the land Caleb wanted. Eighty-five years old, and he wasn't trailing off to play bingo with the other fogies in the lowlands. He wasn't ready to settle down and start looking for some balance in his life. He was taking the hill country. He said:

> Now then, just as the LORD promised, he has kept me alive
> for forty-five years since the time he said this to Moses,
> while Israel moved about in the desert. So here I am today,
> eighty-five years old! I am still as strong today as the day
> Moses sent me out; I'm just as vigorous to go out to battle
> now as I was then. Now give me this hill country that the
> LORD promised me that day. You yourself heard then that
> the Anakites were there and their cities were large and

fortified, but, the LORD helping me, I will drive them out just as he said.[5]

That is an astonishing attitude that we should all want for our lives.

Look, we all go through desert times. We get sucked dry by crappy circumstances or we put ourselves in bad positions and get hurt. Maybe we're not healthy or great things aren't happening for us. We start wandering in the desert in those perpetual Blahs and it can feel hopeless and isolated. Or maybe some squatters have taken over and, as much as we try, it feels like they've got a permanent stake on our land. But that's when we need enduring optimism—that's when we need to look to someone like Caleb and say, "Yeah, I can do it. God's got my back. I can do it." And we keep going.

Great fathering is something that requires endurance and unbalance in favor of your kids. You have to show up every day. You change diapers and try to entertain fussy kids when you'd rather be having a beer while watching a game—and you endure. You might put up with a job that's mediocre because you want food on your family's table—and you endure. You don't get all the cool toys that your friends who don't have kids get to enjoy—and you endure. But someday you will get the blessing of being a great father (or maybe you feel it now). You put one foot in front of the other, you endure, and you do it with optimism because you know that what you're doing is right.

5. Joshua 14:10–12.

Let's be real about something else. If you've been married to the same person for five or ten (or twenty) years, maybe the sex isn't as good anymore. It just isn't. Now it takes more creativity, more work. And you know, that's when some people start looking elsewhere. They look toward that false freedom of lusting after someone else, and that's when crisis hits. But you have to endure. You need to do what's right.

The book of Philippians helps us figure out where to throw our unbalanced weight: "Finally, brothers, whatever is true, whatever is noble, whatever is right, whatever is pure, whatever is lovely, whatever is admirable—if anything is excellent or praiseworthy—think about such things."[6] No matter what circumstance you're in, there's going to be something in it that's true or noble or right or admirable. There will be a choice, and that's when you shake off the "balance" of the world and pursue what you know pleases God.

By the way, for those of us who didn't endure or somebody who didn't endure with us, there may have been great reasons for that. Or if there weren't great reasons, God still gives us grace and forgiveness and continues to forgive as many times as we ask. But for those who are hanging out in the desert right now, wondering if it's worth it to endure, know that it is. It definitely is. You won't have to deal with the unfortunate consequences that come with giving up. Keep pushing, because the best days might be ahead of you, or at least more of the good ones.

In our youth-obsessed culture, we think that if we haven't

6. Philippians 4:8.

experienced amazing things by age twenty-nine we're out of luck. That's crazy. Ray Kroc was fifty-nine when he approached the McDonald brothers with a vision for a restaurant partnership. Before that he was simply selling milkshake machines. Clint Eastwood is producing amazing films at nearly eighty. Caleb was forty when he chose to follow God wholeheartedly and eighty-five when he finally got the hill country.

I don't know where I'll be when I'm fifty-five. When I was twenty, I had no idea I'd be where I am right now at forty-two. I just don't know what the years are going to bring. But what I do know is that statistics show very clearly that if you're aspiring to check out of life at fifty-five to attain "balance," you're twice as likely to die in the few years after retiring than if you just work until you're sixty. So I challenge you to not check out. I'm not charting my life out so that I'll be on the golf course at seventy or playing bingo while eating soft toast. If my physical body needs me to slow down, I will. But if I'm physically fine, I'll keep going. I want the hill country. I want the hard stuff and the best stuff. Freedom isn't cheap, and I want it.

The longer you are wholeheartedly devoted, the longer you endure optimistically, the longer you have humble confidence, the more you have to offer and the more you will be available for receiving God's blessings. You will build up a reservoir of strength and spiritual power. So live unbalanced and plow through the desert. Make choices because they bring you freedom, not mediocrity.

Your greatest days are ahead.

Chapter 12

Live It Out

When I first started following Jesus, people would talk to me about "The Four Spiritual Laws," a sort of religious booklet intended to get people into a relationship with God. I think the objective is to use natural and empirical reasoning as a way to explain who God is and what He offers.

But I never liked those four laws. If the primary thing about figuring out God is learning those laws, then I'd rather not figure out God. Laws restrict. They come with punishment. They are cold and impersonal. These are not the lead characteristics of God. Don't get me wrong: the heart of each "spiritual law" is hard to argue with, but the packaging and precise wording never got me excited.

For example, one of the spiritual laws is "God loves you and has a wonderful plan for your life." When you first hear this statement it sounds great and inviting. It's absolutely true that God does love us and does invite us to a life that makes one separate from Him pale in comparison. But as life goes on, confusion inevitably comes over us. I believe God has a wonderful plan for my life, but what does this mean? Is there only one specific plan or thing God wants me to do with my life? One specific occupation? One specific person to marry? One specific altruistic cause to pursue? Together, these things would comprise my "purpose" and "wonderful plan."

When you're sixteen, this thinking isn't so bad, because you're not yet under the gun. But then at eighteen the stress begins: if you make one bad choice, the "wonderful plan" is jacked up. If you go to the wrong college, you won't be adequately prepared for your chosen career. Likewise, when you start dating, you may become obsessive-compulsive about whether a certain person is "the one." Then if problems arise later—you're unsatisfied in your work or your marriage is particularly difficult—the rational conclusion is that you are outside of God's wonderful plan for your life. Now what? You can't go back in time to make the right decision, but you're in a foreign land with no return voyage. If you don't have a more holistic and biblical approach to your situation, you'll become depressed or bitter and abandon the One who loves you.

You and I are free. We are not in bondage to figure out the one thing that God wants us to do. Every decision before us is not a pass/fail test. If we go through life thinking there is a definitive right and wrong for every decision (or that pain will come our way if we choose the wrong decision—either through bad outcomes or God rapping us on the knuckles), we will go through life with fear and trepidation. We probably won't get very far. However, if we view good options as possibilities that we're free to choose, life becomes more adventuresome and less burdensome.[1]

Here are a few ways that freedom can look when it's lived out.

1. For more on this, read Gary Friesen's *Decision Making and the Will of God* (Sisters: Multnomah Books, 2004).

Freedom in Relationships

When I was in college, I lived with a bunch of Christ-following guys who were training for ministry. (For a snippet of the kinds of stupid things we did, read the section of *Welcome to the Revolution* about us catching arrows we'd shot up into the air.) One of the stupider things I did during that time of my life was mindlessly fall into the assumption that I should be doing what the other guys were doing.

They were all getting married young, so I assumed I should get married young. This meant that every girl I ran across who was halfway decent looking and claimed to follow Jesus was likely *the one*. At this point in my life, I believed that God had one perfect mate picked out for everyone. Some people call this a "soul mate." I now call this a "bad idea."

If you get married and believe that person is the only person God would have been happy about you marrying, your opinion is likely to change about one year into the relationship when you realize there are thousands of other people who would have been just as capable. In my wife Libby's case, there were hundreds of thousands of other guys more capable than I.

The idea that I needed to get married young just like everyone else I knew caused me to ask Libby to marry me in February—after meeting her in September—by dropping her ring in the bottom of a beer glass (I'm a true romantic), and get married in May. As misguided as my marry-young assumption was, and as naive as our dating process was, I hit the jackpot. I took a gamble and won big. I didn't know I was taking a gamble, of course, but I was.

After being married for more than twenty years, doing countless premarital and marital counseling sessions, and interacting with hundreds of other couples who are either happily or unhappily married, I now realize that while spiritual alignment is a prerequisite and sexual chemistry is important, neither makes for a happy married life.

What is the key ingredient above and beyond these things? Being married to a person who is focused on your freedom.

All of us have bruises from the past that require someone to step in and engage. If your parents ignored you as a kid, you need someone who will be willing to pay attention and really listen. If your dad left when you were young, you need to be with someone you can trust to stick around. If you've been sexually abused, you need someone who is willing to go into those dark places with you and offer untold amounts of empathy and affirmation in bringing you to a new arena.

When I'm on my game in our marriage, Libby sees things about herself that she wouldn't see on her own. She has perspectives that she couldn't have arrived at by herself. She senses liberty and gains abilities that transcend her own.

The same is true for me. I have a great life in large part because I have a woman who cheers me on and fights for my freedom. She encourages me to dream big visions, to bite off big projects, and to be fearless in stepping out in faith. In fact, I wouldn't have uprooted my family from lifelong friends and a winning football team in Pittsburgh to move to Cincinnati to help start Crossroads if it weren't for her. When I was offered the job, I said, "I'll have to think about it." (I learned that having cold feet is a literal physiological condition.) But Libby got in my face and said, "What are you hesitant about? This is created for you. You can do this. Let's move." So while some spouses are ruled by fear and won't allow their other half to take career risks or do anything that a life insurance company may frown on, Lib says, "Take your helmet off. Have fun."

You don't have to encourage your spouse in the same way that Libby encourages me. But you need to encourage him or her in some way toward freedom. And if you are dating someone who isn't cheering you on to broad pastures, end it. They need to grow significantly or the rest of your life will be stifled. So do what you need to do.

How many of us got married or started dating someone because we thought that person would make us free? I'm going to guess very few. Maybe we chose him or her because our friends were all in relationships—or we wanted to get laid according to the will of God. But did you stop to ask yourself if that person would fight for your freedom? The people who will fight for our freedom are the people who create options and opportunities for us. We should enter covenant relationships because we can do for others what they can't do for themselves and they can do for us what we can't do for ourselves.

When choosing a person to date, it might be easy to get caught up in the paradigms of what's right, what's wrong, and even the old Christian bracelet favorite WWJD (What Would Jesus Do?). But these paradigms are too limiting in relationships, because WWJD doesn't help me a bit when trying to figure out who to date or marry. Jesus wasn't in my exact situation.

And about sex. Usually we have sex because, in the moment, we feel like it'll be a freeing experience. So we agree to trade our bodies. But ultimately if we're not in a marriage, it only results in memories and emotional carnage that we'll have to spend a long time healing from. It will be something we'll want to hide from the person we truly love in a few years—and that produces guilt and shame. It's the same for affairs. Often people jump at having an affair because it seems to promise freedom and intense excitement. But there is immediate fallout to deal with once it's over, and it becomes clear that it was just a form of false freedom. I'm not just talking about "unwanted pregnancies"—I'm talking about emotional baggage such as rejection, loneliness, worthlessness, anger, and jealousy—to name a few.

Remember the Blahs, the Break, the Blues, and the Blessings? All change, in the moment, can look like failure. So when you choose to stop having sex with someone to whom you're not married, some feelings of abandonment, coupled with dissatisfaction and confusion, will probably settle in. Or if you break up with someone, you might be really lonely when the holidays come. But you have to go through those emotions because that's what freedom usually looks like in the first stages. It looks like it will be worse than what you had before. So you have to hang in there for the blessings, because they, too, will come.

Freedom in Your Job

A friend of mine started a business because he fantasized about making more money, and specifically, he wanted a passive income: one that he didn't have to work fifty hours a week to get. Well, it didn't happen. His monthly cash flow was bleeding dry, and he had to choose whether to tank the entire business and be liable for all the leases and loans he was carrying (thereby losing $150,000) or just keep losing money hand over fist. If you're in a spot like that, I don't think the Bible speaks one way or the other—it doesn't say that you *have* to stick with it, hoping it will turn, or that if you're losing a lot of money every month, you must stop immediately. Either one could be the right thing to do, and you are free to figure it out. Maybe you hope your career turns a corner. Maybe it's the right thing to bite the bullet and end the thing. But what I said to him was, "Right now, what do you think will bring you the most freedom?" He said he had an albatross hanging around his neck, and it was hurting the productivity of every single area of his life. And the thing that would be most freeing for him would be to take the $150K bath. When you add the interest, that's a $750 payment every month for the next thirty years, which his normal income could cover, but he could stomach that because he would know the business had been put to bed. The way he arrived at his answer was to ask himself, "In my day-to-day life, what'll make me most free?"

That's a question to remember.

How many of us chose a career because we thought it would give us a good life for nine hours a day and would provide freedom? Probably most of us chose careers based on salary, health benefits, and ladder-climbing potential. God has wired each of us for tasks and given us spiritual gifts to be successful in completing them. When we choose a career based on income, we're putting ourselves under the taskmaster of money, and that's not a self-freeing choice. (Let's face it: dead presidents make terrible bosses.) A good salary might be a healthy part of your decision, but it shouldn't be the deciding factor.

A lot of people get in a rut while choosing their careers. Fear of choosing the wrong one and then being stuck, or the fear of "Is this exactly the place God is telling me to work?" can put us in a gridlock. But look at how Jesus' close followers made decisions: "It seemed good to the Holy Spirit and to us."[2] They went on journeys and made "career" moves with that outlook.

"It seemed good to us."

If there is something you want to do and it doesn't break any of God's clear instructions in the Bible and will ultimately give you freedom, then just do it. We Jesus-followers love to over-spiritualize common life decisions and make everything very difficult and unwieldy, as if God finds joy in having you fret about everything you do in life. Look, He approves of you as His child, and you can go live your life in freedom. When He speaks to you in an unmistakable way, all bets are off. You obey. But when you have good, truth-honoring options, pick the one that gives you the most freedom. I really believe that it is that simple. Again, "It seemed good to the Holy Spirit and to us." I wish more people understood the freedom and confidence they can have in Christ. And I want that for you. Now.

On a recent fly-fishing trip to Montana, I met a guy named

2. Acts 15:28.

Matt and his father, Don—guys who had left their humdrum lives in Pittsburgh to establish a lodging and fishing-guide business wedged between the beautiful Madison, Big Hole, and Beaver Creek rivers. Many people think about establishing their own business instead of taking marching orders from an employer (who may function as a slave driver). Many think about moving out into the open country away from big-city congestion. Many dream about having an occupation that causes them to spring out of bed instead of just rolling.

Why doesn't this happen more frequently? Because we don't have the stomach for the follow-through. We skip the daily installments because they seem too tedious, or we get distracted by more instant gratifiers. But Matt and Don had an overarching objective that they both were gifted to take on, so they decided to bend their lives to the choice.

Don saved for years while working in the corporate world, living beneath his means and saving the rest. For years Matt studied the intricacies of fishing. His discipline led him to learn that fish see only in black and white. So he did things like go down to the river, capture bugs that the fish were eating, and then take a black-and-white photo of those bugs. Then he would match the strands on his fly to the shades of gray in the picture to lure the fish to jump at his customers' flies versus another outfitter's. Now that's a stomach for follow-through.

Matt and Don bought an old, rundown hotel with their savings and devoted every waking hour to rehabbing it for fishers. If you go fishing with them and find that you aren't doing much catching (that's the only reason to do it, as far as I'm concerned), you're likely to see them pull your one, lonely fish off the line and pump his stomach so that his day's meal comes up onto their hand. Then they'll match one of their hand-tied flies to what was in its stomach. That, my friends, is love for your career.

Since we did more fishing than catching on our trip, I was happy when my nine-hour day in the sun on the lazy river ended. The next day was Matt and Don's day off, and guess what they did with it? They went to a secluded lake to go fishing with family.

Today, if you go to their hotel, you're likely to think, *I could do something like this with my life.* When you say that, Big Don will look at you with squinty eyes long enough to take his cigarette out of his mouth and say, "There are dreamers and there are dream makers."

You are free to make a dream become reality, but don't think that simply having a dream will change anything about your life. Dreams are like freedom. They aren't free. The Bible says (and I think this applies to Matt and Don) that if you're faithful in small things, you will be put in charge of more.[3] So many of us, though, don't pay attention to the small things (like saving money with discipline, putting sweat equity into our dreams, following through with plans, enduring through the Blues, and plugging away at relationships), yet we expect the bigger things to appear for us. It just doesn't happen that way, and it never will.

Another thing to consider if you're already in a career, aren't planning on changing it, and just want to make it

3. Matthew 25:21.

better, is this question: how can that environment be a place of greater freedom? Maybe it's a simple answer. It could be you asking to move away from a negative coworker who is slowly bringing you down; it could be slotting your time into organized chunks instead of multitasking the whole day. If you manage other people, it could mean considering the resources you already have and then literally using what you have instead of always making strategic plans for eight years down the road. For me, freedom as a manager comes when I trust the people I've hired to do their jobs. It sounds simple, but it's unbelievable how many bosses don't do this. If I've hired a guy to oversee the budget, I don't need to be knee-deep in the budget all day. I should use his expertise and give him the freedom to work things out.

If you're an artist, consider that freedom in the creative process is often greatly misunderstood. It's not about "anything goes." All brilliant artists crave boundaries and parameters because they realize that constraints bring freedom. Whether it's the choice of a particular medium or subject matter, or specific objectives for a client, the creation of deeply meaningful creative work demands focus, and focus is about choices. Mature artists realize that every yes will also require them to say no several times if they want to succeed in their efforts and stay healthy and free.

My friend Josh Seurkamp, one of the brilliant artists in my life, describes creative freedom this way:

Watching my kids play in our small, fenced-in yard is one of the best pictures of freedom I've ever witnessed. Inside the confines of the backyard, they dream up worlds full of dragons and castles, and wage battles between the forces of good and evil. There, they feel the safety and freedom to dream and create foolishly.

That's the kind of freedom I crave as an artist. Don't tell me I'm so different and creative that gravity doesn't apply to me. If I jump from a building, I'll fall and die. If you tell me, though, that the same rules apply to me as to everyone else, I'll build a pair of wings that will fly me around the world. That's creative freedom.

When you start making career decisions based on freedom, your life will get a lot simpler and you will be available to be more deeply involved in advancing the Kingdom.

Freedom Versus Aspirations

One of the most astounding sayings of Jesus is, "Take my yoke upon you and learn from me, for I am gentle and humble in heart, and you will find rest for your souls. For my yoke is easy and my burden is light."[4] To hear a lot of preachers talk, it seems like God is only trying to put more regulations and responsibilities on our plates. He isn't. He actually wants to take some things away from us. He is trying to give us a life that won't dig into our shoulders. He wants us to be about things that will make us free.

4. Matthew 11:29–30.

Even though the expectations for our futures are too weighty to bear, we still attempt to shoulder them. Titus, one of my South African friends, once said, "Blessed is he who has no expectations, for he will never be disappointed." When I shared that advice with a large audience, it freaked some people out. It sounds irresponsible or passive; it doesn't sound like the American way. But maybe we should think about it.

Jesus has purchased us and given us our freedom, but that is similar to being given a million-dollar check. The value is in what has been given, but for me to fully enjoy all that it represents, I have to get off my rear, go to the bank, endorse the back, and deposit it into my account. This illustration shows the truth of both sides of the equation of freedom. God gives freely, but we need to move in order to experience it fully.

There is a similar two-sided equation to the relationship between endurance as we're going after a vision and aspiring for something we don't currently have. Just as trying to cash a check that hasn't been signed will lead to frustration, so also going after an aspiration that God hasn't signed off on will rob us of freedom. It takes things like seasoning, spiritual maturity, and the counsel of our community to know the difference between a vision from God and an aspiration from ourselves.

Going after or waiting for such aspirations is a form of bondage. We won't be happy until we get what we want. And then when we do get what we want, we think we can't enjoy it because another aspiration is right on the heels of the last.

If I'm aspiring to have a second house by the lake one day, I'm going to have a hard time enjoying the house I have right now. Even though I definitely wouldn't mind if that lake house happened, once I set it up as an expectation, it sets a lot of things in motion. I have to do research; I have to earn more money; I have to start convincing Libby it's the best thing for us. I'm not talking about being cynical and forgoing dreams. I'm talking about appreciating what you have right *now*. Expectations almost always interfere with that gratitude.

When I was a young dad, I heard that I should pray with my girls at night and also pray for their future husbands— that the men would know Christ and retain sexual purity. I did that for a while; I don't any longer. Why? Maybe it is best for my kids to be single. The apostle Paul makes a compelling case that being single makes you freer under certain circumstances when he says,

> I would like you to be free from concern. An unmarried man is concerned about the Lord's affairs—how he can please the Lord. But a married man is concerned about the affairs of this world—how he can please his wife—and his interests are divided. An unmarried woman or virgin is concerned about the Lord's affairs: Her aim is to be devoted to the Lord in both body and spirit. But a married woman is concerned about the affairs of this world—how she can please her husband. I am saying this for your own good, not to restrict you.[5]

If you're stressed out by hearing, "Blessed is he who has no expectations . . ." maybe you're in bondage to something.

5. 1 Corinthians 7:32–35.

Maybe you have an expectation and you're so freaked out that it won't be met that you can't bear to consider letting it go.

If I'm aspiring to speak at the next big conference, I'll always be jealous when I hear that two friends of mine are speaking there and I'm not. Or if I'm aspiring to have a bigger church, I won't enjoy and appreciate the one I'm in right now. If I'm aspiring to have the newer-model Harley, I won't get lost in the moment when riding the one I have now.

Instead of building your lists of aspirations, it is better to remove barriers and see what happens. Instead of aspiring to be married, remove the barriers that will prevent people from wanting to date you. Develop godly character, develop your mind so you are interesting to talk to . . . and use mouthwash. All of these things will benefit you whether you get married or not.

If you want your business to grow, instead of aspiring for fifty new clients, remove the barriers that prevent clients from coming to you. Notice niches in the marketplace that would be fun, challenging, and fulfilling, and the rest will take care of itself.

I'm not aspiring to retire at sixty-five, but I do remove barriers that will keep me dependent on a consistent income for another thirty years. I remove frivolous spending and am working toward eliminating my mortgage debt. But I won't be slaving around for seventy-five hours a week. (Some people, of course, can work eighty hours a week and it's not unhealthy for them. But when it's hurting their health and people around them, it's bondage.)

Right now, since I'm not slaving for seventy-five hours

a week or planning every square foot of a lake house, I have the ability to take bike trips and spend a week with my kids in Nicaragua. I might not be able to do that at seventy. Aspirations restrict the now.

Freedom in Generosity

One of my friends was getting out of his car recently and noticed a woman standing at the car next to his, watching to see if he'd swing his door open too far and bump into hers. As soon as she believed her Porsche was out of harm's way, she was able to pull herself away from her car and continue on with her day.

Our possessions can immobilize us. We're so afraid they'll break, scratch, or be manhandled that we aren't even enjoying them. They're controlling us, and they give us no freedom. That's the danger of materialism and living a lifestyle that either traps us because we're "living beyond our means" or ties us to possessions that don't bring freedom.

When Libby and I moved from a nice house in Pittsburgh to a two-bedroom apartment in Cincinnati to start Crossroads, we actually felt freer than we'd felt in a long time. When I came home, I could chill and enjoy my family. I had nothing to mow, paint, rehab, or maintain. We had a significant decrease in "comfort" but a significant increase in freedom, including freedom from stress. Our inconveniences weren't important compared to what we were gaining. We knew we were where God wanted us. We weren't in bondage to debt or materialism; we were giving back to God both financially and emotionally.

Freedom comes when you give money back to God (the tithe, or 10 percent, that God asks from us as a starting point). Part of the freedom comes from putting money aside and then knowing how much is left for you to live on. Once you set it aside, you shouldn't have a guilt complex when spending or saving the rest. As we grow in our sense of freedom, it is natural to increase our base amount of percentage giving. And even though we are free to make decisions with the rest, we will still get giddy about giving because we know it will release a burden that someone else is bearing.

My base tip amount is 20 percent. By the way, if you pray before your meal, please do the reputation of Jesus a favor and have a similar baseline tip benchmark. Nothing is worse than someone who advertises Christianity yet is stingy. If you can't afford a generous tip, stay home with Chef Boyardee or just skip ordering dessert. And if you leave a Bible tract as a tip, it's only a matter of time until you get hit by a truck. For some, 20 percent is generous. But what I really love is when I'm served by a single mom and I get to tip 25 percent.

What I love even more is what happened just last week. A couple of friends came to me with a proposition to buy a motorcycle for our friend Josh (the brilliant artist I mentioned before). First, let me give you some background on Josh. He somehow managed to drop out of junior high, has a beautiful wife with four kids, and is a creative and musical genius. Oftentimes artsy types don't make a lot of cash. Such is the case with Josh. Add to that the cost of caring for a family of six, and there just isn't much money left for fun diversions.

Josh does what he calls "motorcycle porn." He logs on to eBay and peruses the motorcycles he would love to buy but can't. In the process, he gets hot and bothered and has a short diversion in the middle of his day. His pick is a 1971 Triumph.

We found out that the bike of his dreams was about two hours away, so we took a drive, put the bike (which didn't run) in the back of my truck, and dropped it off at the mechanic. In the end my gift was $250 to the kitty. That's more than I would spend on my own kids, but I've got to tell you, I was just giddy about this.

On Christmas Day, Josh's wife played a videotape of all of us affirming him as a great man. This took place in front of all of his kids and his father, whom he rarely sees. She walked him out to the garage, and there was his dream bike in perfect running condition. He cried, and I cry just recounting that incident.

There was no tax deduction for that act of generosity, but Josh and all the rest of us felt joy and freedom that put wind in our sails for a long time.

The other part of freedom that comes from generosity is that when you give, money has less and less control over you. Since money has such seductive power, we can easily get sucked into letting it control us. It begins to affect our families, our time priorities, our mental state, and definitely our relationship with God. Hebrews 13:5 says, and I paraphrase, that we should keep our lives free from the love (and false security) of money because we already have a God who will never leave us.

It's also important to set aside a predetermined percentage of income to go to the Kingdom of God. When just starting out, 10 percent is an easy no-brainer. It might not be easy to live on 90 percent of your income, but it is easy to discern that this is what God wants when He says in Malachi 3:8 that when we don't tithe, we're robbing God. Later on, Jesus offers His one word of semi-encouragement to the religious Pharisees when He tells them it is good that they tithe.[6]

As we develop spiritually and financially, it is important to increase our predetermined percentage. Every time I get a pay raise, I go through a process of determining what the new absolute minimum is for giving back to God. Once that number is set, I experience freedom. Again: that's my predetermined minimum, but that doesn't mean I'm stingy with the rest. I feel freedom to spend that money on myself and my family and also feel freedom to throw it around when the mood hits.

I feel good about knowing that I'm about God's work and not my own consumption. I also feel good knowing that if there is a cool trip I can take or a new piece of chrome for my bike that I want and I have the money for, I can buy it. I'm not racked with indecision or guilt about wondering whether I should give more away, because I already went through that exercise in a healthy way.

Don't get me wrong: it is generally a good thing to check our consumerist tendencies. But at the same time, being concerned about whether to enjoy dinner out at a nice restaurant

6. Luke 11:42.

or give that money to someone in Ethiopia can be a source of bondage.

The more that money squeezes a hold of our lives, the more we squeeze God out. When I fixate on my account balances, I become more immune to the people suffering around me. The more I obsess over the latest iPod, the less I'm focused on what God wants to do with my life. I'm not saying that owning an iPod is wrong or that having wealth is wrong; it's when those things consume your daily life that they become an interference with your freedom.

Be free. Live beneath your means. Tip generously. Tithe. Take a vacation.

Chapter 13 ———————

Experience
Community

*C*ommunity is a massive buzzword these days—so much so that it has almost lost its meaning. The word *community* is being used by Internet chat rooms, any group of people with the same career—heck, even the private room at Panera is called the Community Room. But community as I see it (and as it is used in the Bible more than eighty times) isn't something so trite as "Hey, we're all living in the same place at the same time—we're a community!" It's a group of people to whom you *give yourself.* That means that they *really* know you and you *really* know them. You know them well enough to understand what they're good at—you know what their personal gifts are. You also know them well enough to understand their weaknesses—the issues in their lives that have brought them down. Any group of people who can give and receive like that, in love and submission (more on that in a minute), is a true community.

As cool, and in some ways helpful, as online social networking may be, it doesn't come close to being the kind of community that the Bible envisions in setting you up for freedom. Community isn't narcissistically sharing your every thought or your photos from last weekend's party. In fact, no one who is really healthy cares about that stuff or has time to process everything their "friends" are posting. Community isn't everyone who is over eighteen and living in their parents' basement staring at the computer for hours on end. Being in community entails being consistently in tactile, real-world situations where we can learn about each other's strengths and weaknesses while having genuine fun. When that is done consistently with the same people, we taste and bear fruit. In fact, their words to us become like valuable "apples of gold."[1]

The Bible is full of community and stories of people being dependent on others, including Jesus Himself. People get healed together, travel together, and learn together. Spiritual maturity isn't independence; it's interdependence. When you have real needs in your life and fail to tell the people around you, you miss out on their solutions and guidance. When you're struggling to defeat a stronghold, you need people to support you and keep you accountable. When you're learning to be a parent or a new spouse, you need others to tell you how they figured things out.

My friends and I believe in a couple of different versions of community. One is the small-group, pray-and-cry-with-each-other, you-know-my-life's-ambitions-and-dreams community. That's a huge deal. The other is the big-picture community; this is the group of Christ-followers you connect with and about which you say, "What *they're* about, *I'm* about." You do things together as a team that you could never hope to do on your own. I'm a big fan of home-based Bible study and worship groups, but did you ever hear of a house church taking six hundred people to South Africa to do medical clinics for

1. Proverbs 25:11.

HIV-positive patients, build houses for the poverty-stricken, and show love to twenty-five hundred street kids? Yeah. Me neither. But that's the kind of stuff my larger community—not my small group—has done.

I've been meeting with nearly the same group of guys on Monday mornings for eight years. Some weeks and even months seem to be a waste of time, but when I need them they are there and they are priceless. You have to pay to play. Community isn't cheap, but it is more valuable than you can imagine. Libby and I together aren't in an official small group that meets weekly, but we certainly know who our six or so closest couple friends are, and we talk about our pains and our victories together. We also know they are a backstop to us in major times of trouble.

Our macro community is our local church. In that setting there are a lot of people who mean a lot to us. But there are a lot more people whose names we don't know who go there too. And that's okay. Our numbers enable us to form a movement that is taking care of our piece of the mission in the Kingdom of God.

We never knew who Sarah Ranson or Andrew Peters were until we learned they were volunteering in the student ministry that was building into our kids, Lena and Jake. With all the crap kids face today, I can't imagine our family still headed in the right direction without Sarah and Andrew's investment. Candid talk from twentysomethings about things like relationships, choices, and peer pressure have supplemented our teaching in the home. So I pity people who don't make the effort to fit into a larger macro community where blessings can seemingly spontaneously arise to usher in freedom.

Something in us freaks out when people want to know us, *really* know us. A part of us wants to run and hide when people try to get too close to us. Suddenly we feel uncontrollably threatened. FYI, I know what that's like. I've been hurt enough times in my life to want to shy away from deep human contact too. Dealing with people is messy and risky and a little maddening. I think that might be one of the reasons I like motorcycling: I'm out there with this (hopefully) dependable machine, having great experiences and risking nothing, emotionally or relationally. The motorcycle expects nothing of me but the occasional oil change. And I don't have to buy it dinner. I just ride and glide. Simple. Not that there's anything wrong with an emotional vacation, but if you live all of your life like that, you're going down. Let me tell you what I mean.

In the Garden of Eden, Adam and Eve were having a great time together—perfect relationship, perfect openness, and perfect intimacy. But when they listened to the serpent and ate the fruit, they became disconnected. First they became disconnected from themselves (read the story in Genesis 3), and they started down the road of guilt, shame, and fear—as evidenced by how they covered themselves with fig leaves. Not good.

Then Adam and Eve became disconnected from God (they went and *hid* when their best Friend came around), and finally they were disconnected from one another (Adam blamed Eve for his failure). That separation and disconnection had been the plan of the enemy from the beginning (it's part of his stealing, killing, and destroying), and it's still the methodology he uses today. God, on the other hand, is in the business of *uniting* people. He reconnects us to one another, reconnects us to Himself, and makes us whole in ourselves, repairing our psyche and emotional scars. The enemy is about separating you, while God the Father, Jesus, and the Holy Ghost are about bringing you back together.

So for those of us who like to hang out on the fringe with one foot in the shadows, just know that you're in the crosshairs of the enemy. Maybe you don't "like" it, but it's the only place you feel comfortable. You feel vulnerable sharing with a couple of friends? You have no idea how vulnerable you are to spiritual attack when you avoid those conversations.

A place of true community is the place God made for you so that you can really know the free life Jesus offers. If you don't have that, just start asking God for one or two relationships with people who know God and love you and in which you can be real. Notice whom you get energy from and whether those people know Jesus. Start being a blessing to them, and before you know it, you'll find community and the key to freedom.

Once you have this community of six or eight people in your life who love God and know the real you, a natural conversation about your spiritual journey can happen. You can read, talk about, and study the Bible together. You can pray together. You can be a subteam in a big-picture community where you strike out and make a difference in the world around you. But what do you do when those people actually start talking to you about *your life*? What if they say, "Hey, Frank, we've been watching you pretty closely for the past six months, and while it's obvious you have a great heart toward God and care about us, you really have a blind spot when it comes to . . ."?

Submitting to others isn't necessarily what Americans want to deal with or hear about. You'd probably rather give away 20 percent of your income or eliminate caffeine from your diet. Submission, in our culture, implies that someone has beaten you down. You submit when you're weak, inadequate, or without an alternative. At least, that's what we've come to believe. It is what people who aren't free believe.

So who would voluntarily submit to somebody else? I'll tell you: someone who is relationally intelligent and understands the benefit of living within a community and thereby gaining freedom.

A fascinating book called *The Culture Code* by Clotaire Rapaille is about knowing how to sell a product in the midst of the culture you're trying to invade. Rapaille says that if you understand the systems within the culture, you'll be able to better communicate and make the sale. For instance, he describes the rebranding of Jeep. In the early years, Jeep Wrangler sales really floundered. So Jeep brought in Rapaille as a consultant, and his recommendation was to turn the headlights' shape from square to round—a seemingly small adaptation. Sales went through the roof. The reason, according to Rapaille and following studies, was that in the American culture we have a desire for freedom. Round headlights subliminally tapped into the idea of a horse's head and round eyes—running out on the wide-open range—because that's what Americans love: wide-open spaces and the freedom they afford. It is our culture's code, and it helps explain our fascination with independence and resistance to submission in community.

Rapaille calls our culture an "adolescent culture." But *adolescent*, in the way he defines it, doesn't necessarily mean being wrong (or else, clearly, most of my humor would be wrong); it's just a term that helps define the way our culture works:

> Our adolescence stems from one essential point. We never had to kill the king in order to become who we are. Every adult was once a child, small and anxious. And then they go through the stages of adolescence and rebellion. In the American culture, however, our rebellion took an unusual form. Many cultures act out their rebellion by killing their leaders.... We rebelled against the only king who ever tried to rule us and we threw him out of the room.... Our rebelliousness period never really ended.[2]

I don't know how much of what Rapaille says here is 100 percent true, but what I do know is that if you lead anything—a business, a family, a city organization, a committee, anything—you can identify with this: no matter what you do, if somebody wasn't in the room making the decision with you, and he has a stake in the outcome, he probably won't trust the decision. You know that you need a preponderance

---

2. Clotaire Rapaille, *The Culture Code* (New York City: Broadway Books, 2006), 30–31.

of evidence to convince somebody that something is a good idea before he or she accepts it, because Americans naturally tend to distrust people in authority. It is the American way—this way of adolescent rebellion, distrust, and subconscious paranoia.

I fall prey to this rebelliousness. Just last week I was sitting around with some people who were getting ready for a huge, citywide service project. I heard about some of the individual projects happening and thought some of them sounded a little less virile or less intense than others. I sarcastically went, "Gosh, what are we doing that for? Oh, yeah, that will be *real* hard." Then I caught myself. I hadn't planned those 150 or so projects. Very smart people—smarter than me—devoted virtually a year of their lives to researching and planning the whole event, and when I found out about a couple of projects in the span of thirty seconds, I immediately started questioning their judgment. It was ridiculous: a sign of my instinct to distrust and rebel.

Whatever happened to trusting people who make decisions and putting ourselves under authority? Ironically, we are actually limiting our freedom when we refuse to submit. When we don't put ourselves under authority, we aren't being relationally intelligent with other people or relationally intelligent with God. Being submissive to authority increases our freedom, and it builds better community around us.

The theme of submission runs throughout the entire Bible. The fifth and sixth chapters of Ephesians are all about submitting to one another: person to person, employees to employers, Christ-followers to Christ-followers.

When it comes to submitting to your boss, we can look at what 1 Peter says: "Slaves, submit yourselves to your masters with all respect, not only to those who are good and considerate, but also to those who are harsh. For it is commendable if a man bears up under the pain of unjust suffering because he is conscious of God."[3] Some people have inappropriately used and abused this verse to justify slavery. Yet this type of slave-and-owner relationship is not the kind of slavery that was the abomination our own country knows. Our country knows kidnapping—running over to another country, bringing captives back, and forcing labor to bolster our own economy. That is not the kind of slavery that took place in the first century. In the historical context in which this is written, this is more like the debtor's slavery, in which a person would voluntarily put him- or herself in the service of somebody else to pay off a debt. Slavery in this context is not kidnapping or being chained. It is actually about working to a place of financial freedom.

The biblical context is actually closer to an employer-employee relationship—albeit a very difficult one. So what is it saying? When you have a difficult employer, submit. Be aware that you aren't privy to all the things they know, so you have to have some level of blind faith. Honor that person, because when you do, you are honoring the value of authority and are being conscious of God.

Unfortunately, many authorities and spiritual leaders don't believe in you having freedom but rather put stake

3. 1 Peter 2:18–19.

in their own personal perks and their personal desires met through mindless masses. They desire a stable following or growing finances instead of freedom for followers of Jesus. If you find yourself under the authority of someone who constantly looks after him- or herself instead of the cause of Jesus, then that might be a sign that it's time for you to leave that person of authority.

However, be careful of people who constantly find problems with authority and always find a reason to leave their authority figure. In all likelihood, that is the context of someone who is not enjoying true freedom but rather American rebelliousness.

God establishes hierarchy.[4] It's how He organized the world to work. This doesn't mean that God is excited about every person in a position of leadership actually being in that position. It doesn't mean that everybody who holds an elected office is the best person for the elected office. What it means is that the office is something that God uses to govern the world, and therefore we ought to submit ourselves to authorities—whoever they are—and realize that this is God's idea. The Bible says, "Obey your leaders and submit to their authority. They keep watch over you as men who must give an account. Obey them so that their work will be a joy, not a burden, for that would be of no advantage to you."[5] When we submit, the system works. When we don't submit, it doesn't.

But submitting to our authorities isn't just about acknowledging and respecting their positions; it's about how everyone

4. Romans 13; Hebrews 13.
5. Hebrews 13:17.

benefits. If you lead anybody, you know what I'm talking about. When people are constantly second-guessing you, constantly wanting to be heard, constantly doubting or hurling accusations or not doing what's best for the overall organization, it saps the life out of you and keeps you from leading well. And the people you're leading are exhausted. When they're constantly fighting, they can't feel the freedom of giving themselves fully to their role or gifts. The community becomes split, satisfaction decreases, and the grumbling only gets louder.

So what should you do when your community starts to talk to you about your life? Shut your mouth and listen. Submitting to them means that they—by virtue of being the body of Christ and knowing more collectively than you do personally—have a more objective view and can see you better than you can see yourself. If your community says you have a blind spot, you probably do. And may I suggest that God sees your submission to them as obeying Him? Ephesians 5:21 says that we should "submit to one another out of reverence for Christ." And Proverbs 15:31 says that whoever listens to a "life-giving rebuke" is wise. I know it's painful in the moment, but (tired of hearing this yet?) getting freedom can be hard work.

Even though I'm at the top of the organizational chart where I get my paycheck, I do have people to whom I submit: our board of spiritual directors. It's a group of men and women of which I am a part, but I am also in submission to them. As I've thought about my own macro community and the most recent instance in which I had to submit to it, the writing of my first book, *Welcome to the Revolution*, comes to mind. After much research and many lengthy conversations, our board suggested that all the money made from that book—or any subsequent one—should go directly to Crossroads, not to me or through me. It wouldn't even go through my bank account. They asked my opinion, and I'm not suggesting that this is the right choice for everybody, but we decided that the best thing for the mission of our church and for me was for the money to go directly to the church. I could have squawked or haggled about my rights or any other number of self-centered options, but I knew the wisdom of submitting to those who were in authority, and so I did.

Initially, to be honest, I wasn't all that excited about the decision. As a pastor in an American church, having a secondary income stream is a way to stay independent of the church—a way to detach. (Remember how the enemy wants us separated?) I could have done that, but then I would have lost something: my dependence on and collaboration with the community around me. Giving the money straight to the church keeps me grounded and connected. The board was right; they were looking out for the best thing for the Kingdom, the best thing for our overall mission, and therefore the best thing for me.

Submission is when you choose to be "sub" to the mission. You let go of a self-centered focus and forgo complete independence. For many this becomes difficult because they've chosen a mission of personal happiness. You choose your career, spouse, sex life, and daily activities based on what makes you feel best in those five- or fifteen-minute increments, and you absolutely don't want others sticking their noses in your business. Your concern is your immediate pleasure, and you want to protect that at all costs. The benefits of submission, however, almost always come later. It doesn't feel good in the moment because you have to swallow some pride and fight against a distrusting or rebellious spirit. It isn't until later that you see the positive blessings more clearly.

As I've already said, when you live in submission to community, you have people around you seeing things you can't see. That richness in perspective, of course, helps you make better choices. Think about going to a wedding at which the officiant says, "Does anyone know of any reason why these two people should not be married?" And there's that guy in the back row thinking, *Oh, man, I ought to say something. I should have said something way back when they first started dating.* But he didn't say anything because the couple wasn't open to listening and definitely wasn't open to submitting to a friend's opinion, even though he knew them well and could see things they weren't able to see. Nevertheless, his opinion would have been useful to the couple and might have changed their path. When I think of the life lost because people fail to tell one another what they clearly see, for *whatever* reason, it makes my heart hurt. We experience needless pain because we're not in submission to community.

When you honor the authority God has put in your life, you are free of carrying burdens alone and can focus on other things. If you constantly feel obliged to have a say in everything and feel as if you need to make sure people who are in authority over you always get your opinion, then you are focusing on so many different decisions that discernment becomes difficult. It's like multitasking overload: it's not productive. Instead, we should focus on the work that we are uniquely qualified to do. Then we can really drill down on the things that add value to the mission God has for us, both in our micro community and in our big-picture macro community.

This might reveal itself in simple ways. For instance, recently my family had to deal with the whole high school "senior picture" thing. I didn't even know this practice existed. It's awful. Seniors (or rather, their *parents*) go out and spend hundreds, maybe thousands of dollars, flying to Tahiti just to have incredible, *Vogue* magazine–quality photos taken. Crazy. Whatever happened to the good old days of standing in front of a chalkboard? Now *there's* a school photo I can believe in— and afford! Well, my oldest daughter needed senior pictures, so we started talking about it. Thankfully, her friend found a good and reasonably priced photographer. This friend's family are people I know, and they're very financially responsible, so I just submitted to the decision they'd made for their own daughter. Libby and I didn't need to go through the yellow pages and double-check this and that. Instead, we trusted someone else's decision making, which is a form of submission. Although those parents aren't our formal authority on an org chart, we still submitted.

Following this practice when we can makes life a whole lot simpler. Now with my saved time, I'm able to do things like break down game tape of the defensive sets of my precious Pittsburgh Steelers. See how that works? A Christmas miracle.

When you submit to others, community is benefited and life starts to work.

Last year I was in Mamelodi, South Africa, when I was reminded again of the American resistance to submission and how other cultures operate much differently. I was helping out a team doing eye care by doing crowd control in a room the size of a racquetball court. It was a holding tank for kindergarteners and first graders—about two adults to every one hundred kids. Rows of chairs were set up in a U-shape around the room, and all these itty-bitty African kids were waiting to go, one by one, into the eye-care office. No air-conditioning. No video rolling to keep them occupied. The kids just sat there waiting their turn—no tears, no tantrums, just happy kids. They respected the authority of the adults in the room and were thankful to be there.

I talked to my friend Titus about how his culture responds to submission. Now, we're talking about a culture that has undergone apartheid, where they lived with dominant, overbearing, ungodly people who physically subverted them. But Titus's response was that even though they had survived difficult conditions, they were brought up having chiefs, community leaders, and spiritual leaders they looked up to. A new government didn't change their instinctual response. Titus says they have a saying that goes, "You are a person by others. You are made who you are by other people." That makes me want to be even more diligent in stemming the rebellious tide that has swept over our nation.

For the sake of our real freedom, I want everyone in our nation to see that authority can be *good* and helpful. May you be more South African than American in your attitude and behaviors with regard to rebellion versus submission.

*

I have been living for a while now with the decision to submit to my authorities and forgo all profits from my first book. You know what? My authorities were right.

I'm supposed to submit not just when I agree with the decision made, not just when I have a personal relationship with those in authority, and not just when I am assured that they have all the facts as I see them. I'm simply to submit, realizing that they have information and perspectives I don't have, and that they have responsibility before God for those decisions. That makes them qualified to lead me.

A few great things have happened since I submitted to that decision—things I couldn't have anticipated. First, I have been able to lean into other gifted staff members who have helped my writing get to another level. I'm not great as an individual; I'm a good team guy. I need to be around other people during a project in order for my A game to come alive. Since Crossroads is getting the money, I'm free to use some staff to help form a writing team. Were it not for that, Liz Young—who has a master's degree in writing—wouldn't be making my bad grammar and variant thoughts readable. I never saw that coming.

I also didn't anticipate how excited the rest of the staff and church would be that I wasn't on the traditional "megachurch pastor superstar" track. So, in forgoing a fatter bank account,

I was showing that I wanted to live in interdependence on our community. I don't aspire to be a spiritual lone ranger. All great things in the Kingdom happen in a team context. By being financially dependent on our church, I'm living out what I constantly say: that I'm all in.

I also didn't anticipate how Crossroads receiving the profits from the book would encourage financial generosity. I've heard people say, "When Brian talks about tithing, I now know that he has more understanding of what I'm up against, because before he only tithed on what I've given him. Now he has other earned money he is willingly giving up."

Crossroads pays me a very generous salary, for which I am very thankful. Since they take care of me and since I am not growing my lifestyle according to additional advances and royalties, I'm not driven to "publish or perish." I feel no bondage to write another book. And it's a good feeling. My decision to submit led me to a level of freedom I wouldn't have experienced otherwise. So you see that, for me, submission to community has produced a variety of good fruit that might be mistakenly attributed to me. But it really wasn't me; I was just in agreement with God's system of living under proper authority. And you know what, friends? It feels really good. Freedom always does.

It can be a life-altering thing to tell just a few friends around you, "Hey, I realize that God has brought you into my life, and it's not just so we can drink beers together. I need your input in every part of my life: my significant-other relationship, my eating habits, my walk with God, my career, and yes, my grooming habits. I need to be in submission to people like you!" And if you have felt God's Ghost inside you saying, "Yes! Yes!" as you read my description of the American sense of rebellion and independence, it might be a great idea for you to pray right now and be done with all that stuff for good. If you get into right relationship with the authority in your life (and I mean *all* authority: civic, governmental, church, familial, and work related), new levels of enjoying God will be right around the corner for you.

God has given us freedom to make decisions in our lives—but He hasn't given us freedom about whether to submit to authorities. We are bound by this command when we choose to follow Jesus. And the crazy thing is that even when we are bound by commands, they are the kind of shackles that lead to freedom.

Chapter 14 ——————————————

When Grace Meets Truth

When I got into the biker scene a few years ago, I realized that I came alive when I was on the open road with my American-made steel horse under my rear end. It isn't just being out in the middle of beautiful creation; it's the whole experience. Please keep in mind that I'm a married father of three who owns a minivan and loves Carrie Underwood. Translation: I'm not a rebellious hellion. But when I get on my bike, I take on a different persona. For me, putting on biker gear and hitting the road is like Halloween for a little kid. I wear things I normally don't wear, I go places I normally don't go, and I ingest things I normally wouldn't consume. I feel like a different person. Not a middle-aged minivan driver but a real Man's man. The kind who goes barefoot all winter, kills a moose with his bare hands, and opens a beer bottle with his front teeth. Yet, it seemed as if the one thing that every true biker possessed that I didn't possess was a tattoo.

However, I had three problems to figure out. First, would the needle in the tattoo parlor be able to penetrate my rock-hard, minivan-driving biceps? Second, was there anything I would put on my body that I wanted marking me for the rest of my life? Third, what about that Bible verse that says tattoos are a bad thing?

Leviticus 19:28 says, "Do not cut your bodies for the dead or put tattoo marks on yourselves. I am the LORD." This is a law, and since I'm not an Antinomian, I take these instructions seriously. Antinomians, by the way, are anti-law guys (*anti* meaning "against," *nomes* meaning "law"). In the church's history, antinomians were accused of encouraging people to go against God's moral standards. Today they believe that things like the Ten Commandments are irrelevant. They don't think they should be held up as the ultimate standards of a life devoted to God. Antinomians are also often accused of abusing grace. So, just for the record, I'm not an antinomian. I aspire to keep the Ten Commandments simply because God commanded me to, I do my best to obey the Bible because I've submitted myself to the ultimate authority of God, and I trust my life will be the better for it—since God doesn't give restrictions for restriction's sake. I also see a bunch of other absolutes in the Bible that I break only to my peril.

So regarding what the Bible says in Leviticus, it's obvious to me why someone shouldn't be a cutter. Fortunately, I'm not drawn to that practice. But the Bible also seems to say that tattoos are off-limits.

As I dug into the meaning of this verse by looking at the context—both historic and literal—I discovered that pagan religions of the time encouraged branding in their worship of dead ancestors. The branding could be done through cutting and creating a brand through scar tissue or through puncturing the skin with something that contained ink—thereby creating a tattoo. When people would do this in worship of the dead, they definitely weren't worshipping God. This is why God finishes the instruction by saying, "I am the LORD." Not your dead ancestor, but Me.

After studying the context, it became obvious to me that tattoos aren't inherently an offense to God, though some could be. (The Playboy bunny, let's say, would be a bad choice.) So the question becomes, what statement will I be sending to others and to God? Who am I willing to align my life with? If I was to align myself with something opposed to the real God and the tattoo was a marking of that intention, I would definitely be breaking God's law. I wasn't planning to go that route.

So the only problem was finding something that I was willing to mark myself with for life. After racking my brain, I couldn't come up with anything, so I let the tattoo idea die. Then one day I was reading about Jesus' life as described by His friend John. (This is known as the Gospel According to John.) John writes that Jesus came to earth "full of grace and truth."[1]

When someone has a strong personality and is unwavering, we might say, "Bill is stubborn as a mule." If someone is conceited, we'll say, "She's full of herself." I've known some people to be "full of passion." These kind of statements are meant to be CliffsNotes that describe the overarching theme of someone's life. Jesus' theme was being full of grace and truth. What's so strange about this statement is that the words *grace* and *truth* are rarely put together when describing someone. They seem to be a contradiction. Yet they lead to freedom.

Those known as Grace People cut others a lot of slack. They're the ones you want to be around when you've cheated

1. John 1:14.

on your wife or need justification for acting out of anger. On the other hand, Truth People put others on a tight leash. They're the ones you want around when you're confused and need solid, concrete direction.

- Grace people major in compassion and tend to see the good in everyone. Truth people major in passion and tend to see the good in obedience.
- Grace people have time for those who need another chance. Truth people want to help you in your decision so you don't need another chance.
- Grace people see the bad in restriction. Truth people see the bad in relative morality.

You can see that none of these statements are negative. We need all that grace has to offer and all that truth has to offer. Yet, experienced separately, grace and truth won't offer freedom and will eventually oppress both the giver and the recipient. Exclusive grace won't help you or others make sound decisions or honor God. Exclusive truth will leave us cold and tired—and won't woo anyone to God. But taken fully together, grace and truth keep us on the road to wholeness; they're the guardrails that keep us from wrecking our lives with either legalism or antinomianism.[2]

Merging grace with truth is a significant shift in thinking for both the world's systems and the typical Christian systems.

2. For more on the guardrail illustration and a deeper look at grace and truth, I highly recommend Randy Alcorn's *The Grace and Truth Paradox* (Sisters: Multnomah Publishers, 2003).

Both systems usually lean to one extreme or the other, and neither does a good job of giving out grace and truth fully.

How can we embody both? Sometimes, being full of grace and truth is like using a toggle switch: you occasionally flick to being all one or all the other. When interacting with friends who are having adulterous affairs, it is at first full truth. I say things like, "You need to stop this right now. God is not happy. This is going to hurt a lot of people." In those unfortunate situations when a friend persists and gets a divorce, I've actually gone to people and said, "I am choosing to give you grace and not speak to this issue anymore. You are my friend, regardless of what you do."

On the other hand, sometimes the grace/truth mix is like a fader: we give a percentage of grace and a percentage of truth in a specific interaction. It could be 50/50 or 90/10 or 10/90. But if we are weighted the same way in every situation, then we aren't full of grace and truth. We're just being habitual.

Jesus, the ultimate Freedom Giver, didn't come to earth with diluted grace or half-hearted truth. He came with full 100 percent industrial-strength grace and 100 percent no-compromise, in-your-face truth. No wonder He is so extraordinary. No wonder He astounds people to this day. No wonder Napoleon Bonaparte said of Him: "Everything about Christ astonishes me. His spirit overwhelms and confounds me."[3]

Here's some truth: we all deserve immediate hell for the way we've offended a loving, holy, and pure God. How badly have I offended God? I've lied, dishonored my parents, stolen,

3. Alfred Holmes, *Life Thoughts from Pulpits and Poets* (Published by the author, copyright 1874), 223.

and masturbated to the image of people made in the image of God. I could fill pages and pages with my transgressions. And that would be just a week's worth. Yet here I sit in my beautiful, air-conditioned home with an incredible family and life generally going my way. Every good and perfect gift comes from God.[4] So even though my natural rebelliousness toward God when I go my own way is a result of me being "dead" in my transgressions—meaning I'm unable to please God in and of my own power—His grace comes to the rescue and makes me alive.[5] That's the full-strength grace God gives, and that's one way He gives me freedom. I've been forgiven and released—not because I earned a clean slate, but because He loves me.

There's one thing you should know about what happens with grace: many people might raise an eyebrow or get ticked off when you're experiencing it or giving it. Freedom can make people nervous and judgmental. You'll be under the gun. But that's a good sign, because until somebody is uncomfortable with the grace you're giving in different situations, you're probably not giving enough.

For some reason it seems people prefer that we live with our mistakes—that we hang out in the dusty confessional booth and have time to "do penance" and suffer the consequences for our sin. People who fill churches and even read Bibles often fall into this category. Galatians 2:4 says that these people sneak into our meeting "to spy on the freedom we have in Christ Jesus and to make us slaves." In other words, your freedom can cause some intense jealousy.

4. James 1:17.
5. Ephesians 2:1–6.

When our house caught fire and literally destroyed all our family had, we felt a lot of judgment from people in our previous church. We hadn't purchased fire insurance, and a lot of our friends were helping us out with clothes and money. We were getting grace from our friends, and some didn't like it— saying we were being "rewarded" for a "bad decision." That's the ugly underbelly of the situation, and it was very traumatic for us to feel how people often choose judgment over grace. Yet if you're able to live out the beautiful, intense, and unlikely unification of grace and truth, you'll find freedom.

Look at Jesus: He was accused of being a glutton and a drunkard. Why? Because He was giving grace and living a grace-filled life with wine and great food. The president of the Bible-thumping society may never get accused of being a glutton or drunkard, because he doesn't live close enough to grace. This goes back to the problem of having an all-truth focus. If you don't combine grace and truth, you'll never woo others to the God who gives freedom.

When you add truth to your grace, of course, you'll still be accused. Truth can make people uncomfortable—really uncomfortable—and that's why it's so important that you also embody genuine grace. When we speak truth, we must be willing to live with some accusations and defensiveness. Although Jesus was accused of being a drunkard and glutton, He was also disliked for invoking higher standards in divorce and having a higher morality by saying adultery is not just a physical action but also a mental and emotional one,[6] likewise with murder.[7]

6. Matthew 5:27–28.
7. Matthew 5:21–22.

So being a truth- and grace-giver isn't always accepted, but it's the model Jesus gave and the way to freedom for us and for others.

*

Reader, beware: what follows are thoughts on the g-word. While confrontations on sensitive issues can make your stomach turn, they also have the power to open us up and push us into greater freedom. Here's a case in point.

Recently I publicly interviewed a guy who talked about his homosexuality and the effort it took to change his behavior and the renewal he found in doing so. After the interview two lesbians pulled me aside to ask me what I was trying to encourage by asking this guy to tell his story in front of everyone in the church—was I trying to force them all out of being true to their desires? One of my close family members is a lesbian, so I've had similar conversations before. What I say to her, and what I said to these women in the manner of truth and grace is, "Hey, I love you, and my love is really unconditional. *And* I think there's a better way you can live your life." That didn't comfort the lesbians. One said back, "My partner here—this is her first time in church." And the whole time she's talking, the other woman is crying. So I'm left to wonder, is she crying because God's Spirit is touching her and she's being overwhelmed? Or is she crying because she's afraid she's being judged and going to hell?

I think what the women were expecting was one of two

responses: "Hey, go for it. Just live how you're living and receive 100 percent grace," or "Oh, I'm sorry, hell awaits you, and you're not welcome here." But what they got from me was, "There's a better way you can live your life *and* we're excited you're here. You might disagree with me on things I say—a lot of people do—but I'm still glad you're here."

Homosexuality is such a lightning-rod issue that I'm sure I'll invoke judgment and misunderstanding for bringing it up. Yet for us to look at the book of Romans in the Bible and the theme of freedom as it ties to truth and grace, we have to acknowledge the first chapter in Romans, which deals mostly with homosexual sex; it's referred to as not being "natural." Natural things have the capacity to reproduce. If gay men and women were on separate islands, the effect would be zero births and an eventual end to the human race. Still, many will persist in having unnatural sex, and God doesn't withhold all forms of freedom in the lives of people living that way. He will "give them over"[8] to that urge—that is, they will be free to go after that practice without the pangs of guilt they may have felt in their first few sexual encounters—just like the pangs of guilt I feel the first few times I do anything I'm not designed for.

This isn't just about homosexuality; it's about first indiscretions and continued indulgences in things we aren't designed for, such as using porn, hoarding our money, spreading gossip, lying on our income tax return, and so on. At first these indiscretions usually bring some guilt, but we push the guilt or questioning aside the more we do it. It begins to feel

8. Romans 1:26.

less dirty. Five days into the unnatural behavior we're starting to forget our guilt. Twenty days later it's pushed aside. Before you know it, even our physical chemistry has been adjusted. It's like the tenth time we've swallowed a whole chocolate cake: our body is ready to accept it; the stomachache isn't quite as bad. One thing I can get "given over" to is throwing out biting, sarcastic comments. After a while, if my sarcasm goes unchecked, I won't feel bad. I'll be at the height of my sarcastic game.

Here's the sliver of freedom in those things: God allows us to mask our pain. He gives grace. Maybe we're downing a fifth of vodka to mask our memory of abuse or overbuying possessions to cover a feeling of inadequacy. Maybe we're hoarding our money and avoiding tithing because a church hurt us in the past and we are masking that old pain. The masking provides some freedom—we're no longer feeling pain 24/7. If we had to live with the full weight of our guilt every day, it would immobilize us. So God gives us this form of freedom as a blessing, even though a stronghold is keeping us from ultimate freedom. So we need people who will speak truth against what we're doing that's holding us back. Just like I needed someone to tell me my e-mail to "Jerk Face" wasn't appropriate, you might need someone to point out that the way you manipulate the truth to "get ahead" at work is keeping you in bondage. Or maybe this book is that truth-giver for you.

When I talked to the two lesbians that weekend, I was not attempting an easy out. I wasn't just trying to be the nice guy. The freedom perspective is about a separate, third position. It has a different plot, and this new plot takes some rethinking, because we're used to moving within certain circles or paradigms (even if we pride ourselves on thinking outside the box). We want exact, clear answers so that we can either safely agree or self-righteously criticize. But to consider another paradigm entirely? That takes some breaking down of old ways and systems. And if you have been bound up by religion and rules and fear, get ready for change.

Merging truth with grace might not be a natural thing for you. Maybe you dislike making any sort of confrontation or risking hurt feelings, or maybe you live off subtle condemnations while talking about others who are "messing up." Whatever camp you fall into—especially if you're on one extreme or the other—try adding from the other side.

Consider how Jesus lived. He hung out with the outcasts—the people who sinned and did horrible things and carried big burdens. He also hung out with people who had really committed to a healthy way of living and were more "on the right track." He didn't shun either side; He embraced both. Jesus was about blessing and engaging everyone. Of course, when He mingled with the big-time sinners, the prideful ones in the crowd were not happy at all. They wanted Jesus to judge the addicts, the partiers, the criminals. But Jesus knew that the ones with the open minds were the ones who knew they needed Him and needed to change something in their lives to get closer to the freedom He offered. They were humble enough to ask for it. The teachers of the law, the "holy"? Not so. In their frustration and blame, they were threatened. They didn't feel freedom, so they didn't want others to experience it either.

Consider the Christian who is ticked off because some guy on death row accepts Jesus at the last minute—really accepts Him—and is given the same blessing the Christian will get. The Christian says, "Hey, I've lived my life by the rules. I've sacrificed things and witnessed to others and taken the hits. The guy on death row should suffer and go to hell." Well, the guy has suffered. His life has probably sucked. Instead of condemning him and saying it's unfair, the Christian should be thrilled that God is so willing to extend grace. Even if he has eternal freedom, he didn't experience the joy of freedom on earth as God desired.

One of my worst childhood memories is when I was playing "Midget Football." (I know that sounds bad, but it was the official name of the league.) I was nine or ten, and there was this guy, Dale, who played on my team. For whatever reason, Dale was one of those kids who got taunted relentlessly. After practice one day, when nearly everyone had left and there wasn't any adult supervision, the remaining two guys began pushing Dale around. It got really bad. They had him down on the ground punching him in the back and spitting on him. I didn't join in, but I stood there and didn't defend him. His dad finally showed up and no one confessed. I felt—and still do feel—like a weak little boy with no backbone.

God wants us to be rescuers—people who tackle oppression and give freedom to others. We're exposed to all the good news of Jesus' life and example for living, and we need to take that as a model and go forward so others experience His goodness too. Oppressed people liked being around Jesus; they should like being around us.

When the Civil War was ending, Abe Lincoln got in the fray. He wanted to be in enemy-occupied territory, inside the controversy where documents were being signed, because he needed to make a statement. When the slaves saw Lincoln, they fell down and praised him. Lincoln told them to not do this, but when people experience freedom from a rescuer—when God chooses the rescuer and works through him—it's hard to separate that person from God. Freedom is that powerful. People run after it, and they fall to their knees when it's found.

How can you be a freedom-giver? Freedom-givers are marked by these things:

- They free the oppressed, sometimes even physically.
- They err on the side of grace.[9]
- They cheerlead other people's freedom and don't just keep it to themselves.

I have someone who champions my freedom by balancing truth and grace: his name is Brian Wells. We're extremely different. I'm not all that interested in safety, but I've known Wells to set his security alarm while he's out shoveling his driveway. Wells doesn't smoke an occasional cigar or drink a few beers, and I like both. Since we live next door to each other, he sees this stuff I do and I see the stuff he does. And I think he thinks some of the stuff I do is wrong. He might even wonder if I'm sinning when I do some of these things.

9. Romans 14.

But what he says is, truthfully, "I'm not sure. And I'm going to give Brian Tome grace."

You want to be around freedom-givers. You don't want to be around partisans, judges, control freaks, or the arrogant.

You are part of a team. You are intended to be God's hands, God's feet, God's extension of love. You were not meant to just accumulate stuff for yourself and simply do what feels right. You are meant to be an unleashed freedom fighter.

If you have kids, how do you give freedom to them? Maybe you never tell them, "You can be anything you want to be," because that's not freedom for them. That line makes them think they should be able to handle everything and tackle, literally, any goal—whether they're designed for it and whether it will lead them to a healthy place. Instead, call out the specific gifts of your children. You see what they don't see, so share what you know.

Do the same for your friends and people you interact with. Tell them the truth about what you see in them. Give them freedom by telling them what gifts they have and where and how they are making an impact. And then whatever you can do to contribute to their freedom—whether that's helping them sort through an unhealthy relationship, forgiving them when they hurt you, or stepping into a midget football fight—do those things with truth and grace.

*

In processing the power of grace and truth, I revisited the tattoo idea, deciding I'd like to be known and forever marked as a person full of grace and truth. What emerged was the image below, which is currently inked on my shoulder.

Grace and truth are the yin and yang of Jesus; they hold together and are in equal dependence. The crown of thorns Jesus wore on the cross? That is the absolute epitome of full grace and full truth.

When truth and grace merge, they become a combination that requires an alternative way of living. It's difficult, uncomfortable, and beautiful all at the same time. I encourage you to try it.

Chapter 15

The Crash

Okay. It happened. This is the chapter I never planned to write, but now I have to write it. After reading the first chapter of this book, many of you might have discredited me or decided I was just stupid for not wearing a helmet when I ride my motorcycle. Well, now it's even worse. I just wrecked.

Four of us decided to rent Harleys out West for an eight-day, multistate ride that would also include a little fly-fishing if we needed a change of pace. For most of the trip I slotted myself in third place in the line of bikes. This particular morning ride was beautiful. Rolling hills, rocky mountains, amber waves of agriculture, tight turns, wide-open straightaways. We had perfect terrain, perfect weather, and perfect riding partners. All was good. We clocked about one hundred miles by the time we pulled in for a 10:00 a.m. breakfast sandwich in a little town that reminded me of Louis L'Amour western novels (with a twentieth-century upgrade).

As I sat eating my breakfast sandwich, I realized the only problem with the morning was that I spent more time ensuring the proper distance between my bike and the one ahead of me than fully enjoying the scenery. What I like about riding is feeling that I'm a high-plains drifter lost in my own world. When I'm concentrating too much on how those around me are riding, it takes something away from the experience.

So when we headed out again, I took off in the lead. This is acceptable biker protocol as long as you don't make a turn without waiting for the rest of the group to catch up.

The next twenty minutes were heaven on earth. My wish was granted, and I was lost in the ride. Not only was the scenery fantastic, but so were the roads. There were climbs with sharp turns that looked out over the flatlands, valleys with meandering curves, and full-out straightaways that afforded speed.

I was riding fast but also trying to ride smart. I was toward the centerline of my lane, since people darting out into the road is a real danger and the extra three feet could make the difference. I was watching for fine stones on the turns. Unless I could see two turns ahead, I was well within the tires' ability to grip the road while leaning in. When I came up to crests, I slowed down, not knowing what was on the other side.

Feeling free, lost in my own world and basking in God's glory, I was coming down a road with a slight grade that was a dead straightaway with few signs of civilization except for the posted sign of the 70 mph speed limit. On the right was a split-rail fence partially hidden by a bushy tree.

And then it happened: a deer jumped out from behind the tree onto the white line. I tried to apply the brakes, but it was hopeless. I knew collision was inescapable. There was no time to pray. There was no time to have fear. There was a thud, and then I was rolling on my side—rolling like a kid going down a grassy hill—except back then I had some sense of control. On the pavement rolling over 70 mph, there's no control.

With my hands tucked to my chest, with each revolution, I kept saying to myself, *Watch your head.* But while I was aware of my head, in reality there was nothing I could do. I had no control over what was happening, only awareness.

The police report says that from the point I hit the deer to where I stopped rolling was sixty yards. I don't know how long I was airborne, but if I was in the air for twenty yards and rolling for forty, then I did about thirty revolutions in about ten seconds.

When I stopped rolling, I stood up to survey the damage, and I thought, *For sure adrenaline's masking my injuries, but I think I'm good.* I felt all my limbs, and they didn't seem to be broken, and my head seemed okay too. My hands were filled with blood, all right, but it wasn't from my head—it was from the pavement tearing into my palms. (If your stomach is a bit squeamish, you may want to skip ahead a few paragraphs.)

Then a local angel pulled up in her car: Christine Brown. She knew something was wrong when she saw deer entrails in the middle of the road followed by a trail of blood up to my dead would-be assassin on the side of the road. Twenty yards further was my mangled motorcycle. Flies were swarming all over it, since it was coated with all sorts of fresh food. It was hard for me to see all of this until I took off my sunglasses and noticed the problem. My lenses were coated, as was my coat, with various deer matter. I learned then that at 75 mph a motorcycle will cut a deer in half. It's not a clean cut, but the end result is the same.

My three friends showed up on the scene along with a state trooper. I kept answering his questions in a vague and defensive manner, concerned that more trauma was on the way. Finally, he said, "Sir, you are not in trouble. You did nothing wrong. I just have to fill out my report." That made me feel a little better. Then the angel Christine offered to drive me to the local hospital. As I walked to her car, I had my first overwhelming sense of God's presence.

I find myself regularly wanting more of God, and that often means wanting more of the miraculous or more signs of His presence. When I hear about other people having intense visions or dreams from God or speaking in languages they have never learned, I admit: I'm jealous. (That's one of the squatters I've got to evict.) For instance, a woman from our macro community was teaching music in South Africa for a week, and at the end of her time, one of the students (through a translator) thanked her not only for her great insights but also for speaking in Zulu. She promptly said through the translator, "I don't speak Zulu." The student said, "For the past week you have been speaking our native language." This is the spiritual gift of tongues that is seen in the Bible's book of Acts. While I've been spiritually abused for not having this gift, I can't deny that things like this are real and I'd love to have more experiences that are outside my normal ones.

When I hear about some people's spiritual experiences or read real-life happenings in the Bible, I regularly think, *I want that. I want to experience Your fullness in ways that surpass the natural order of things.* I don't think that is a bad desire. But I do think it is bad when we believe that in the absence of these occurrences God is holding out on us. God never holds out on us. He allows us to experience what is best, and only He knows what is best. He knows how each of us needs to experience freedom.

Recently I'd been in one of those "I want more" phases, which had crept close to aggravation with God. As I walked toward Christine's car, I paused and tearfully said, "No more, God. I'm not going to expect anything more than what I just got today. If You want to give me more, that is great, but what happened today is Your miraculous gift to me. It is just between You and me. No one I've known has ever ridden 70+ mph without a helmet and been thrown sixty yards and walked away without a scratch on their head. Thank You. You are so good."

For most of the rest of the day, I was in the hospital being checked out and cleaned up. All the seams on my leather jacket had been ripped out. Snaps on my chaps and jacket were ground down from the force and friction of the road. Some were pinched as if they were in a vice. Seams along the heels and ankles in my brand-new boots were separated. The seat of my jeans was ripped out.

As they had me strip down to check every inch of my body (lucky them), they found singed blue jean fibers embedded in my posterior. The heat from the friction of forty yards of asphalt can do amazing things.

By the end, I had a total of seven stitches on my left two knuckles and a smattering of Band-Aids. I didn't need an X-ray, and I didn't have so much as a literal scratch anywhere on my face or head.

When the hospital staff left my room so I could put my clothes back on, a song came flooding to my mind that had been on my iPod. I raised my hands and spontaneously sang in worship to God.

> *We stand and lift up our hands*
> *For the joy of the Lord is our strength.*
> *We bow down and worship Him now.*
> *How great, how awesome is He.*
> *And together we sing . . .*
> *Holy is the Lord God Almighty.*
> *The earth is filled with His glory . . .*[1]

In the days following the accident, numerous people said, "Brian, you were lucky." I was quick to correct them. "No," I said, "I am blessed, not lucky. What happened wasn't by chance. It was the intentional decision of a powerful and merciful God." It was an intentional decision for my life. I'm not sure why there hasn't been an intentional intervention by God in other matters pertaining to my life or the lives of others, but we need to celebrate whatever free gift comes our way without questioning the fairness of it all.

As we have talked about, God has created a world in which free choices run their course. He can and does step in periodically to change the natural consequences arising from someone's chosen course of action. Walking away from my accident is one such example. Another could be ensuring that the weather is perfect for an important day when the natural barometric pressure and wind patterns were going to bring

---

1. Chris Tomlin, "Holy Is the Lord," EMI Christian Music Publishing, 2003.

a storm. Another could be allowing Britney Spears to have yet *another* hit record. But no one can explain why people holier and more deserving are not spared of cancer, why tsunamis aren't always diverted, or why the pure-hearted and talented singer-songwriter can't get a record deal. There isn't a predictable rhyme and reason to such instances. The best I can say is, "We all grieve for the natural course of pain that came your way or the way of your loved one."

The other thing people said often about my accident was, "You should have worn a helmet." "No," I said, "I should have worn gloves."

Here's where you might dismiss me, but I'm holding my ground. I do not recommend that people ride without a helmet. I do not think less of people who wear helmets on a motorcycle. I do think it is a valid criticism that I am not cautious enough. But none of those things presupposes that God is angry with my decision or that I am not free to make this decision.

Freedom means I am free. Free to do things that aren't against the law. Free to do things I'm able to do. Free even to do things that are dangerous. My grandmother said, "Cleanliness is next to godliness," but God has never said, "Safety is next to godliness."

Not wearing a helmet is a calculated risk that isn't any more sinful than having only 5 percent equity in your house, having your first child at forty, smoking cigars, or starting your own business. I think you're stupid if you only have 5 percent equity in your house, but that isn't sinful. God isn't anti-mortgage, and in certain situations a mortgage may be wise. You can think I'm stupid if you want, but don't confuse that with me being sinful.

The Bible says, "God gave us a spirit not of fear but of power and love and self-control."[2] Can you not see that your fears of what could happen are keeping you from what could be?

How many people do you know firsthand who have cancer? Not those you have heard about, but those you actually know? How many people did you know firsthand who died in a car accident? How many people did you know firsthand who died on a motorcycle? We are so often afraid of things we haven't seen firsthand. The fact that we have such intense convictions about things that rarely happen is more evidence of the insidious plan of the evil one to keep us restricted through fear in our life choices, instead of freely exercising choice in areas where God has given us freedom. The world's culture has built this into us, and at a great cost. We become nervous, paranoid, guarded people.

Imagine that in front of you are fifteen bottles tagged for the previous fifteen years of your life. In each of those bottles are folded strips of paper. Those bottles contain all the fears of those years.

Go ahead and revisit the fears, and almost without exception you'll find that they didn't happen. In fact, you have probably forgotten about them.

Bottle 1999 contains Y2K: it didn't happen.
Bottle 2006 contains the bird flu: it didn't happen.
Bottle 2009 contains swine flu; I'm still eating bacon.

2. 2 Timothy 1:7 ESV.

In my bottles are these fears:

- My daughter was going to get sexually abused at a neighbor's house. She didn't.
- Staff members would take me to court out of spite. They didn't.
- My son would break his neck in a football game and be paralyzed. He didn't.
- The tickle in my throat was cancer. It wasn't.
- Our church would fold under financial pressure. It didn't.
- I would run out of passion for preaching and would have nothing of value to say. I haven't.
- A deer would jump in front of me ...

The crazy thing is I never imagined that one happening. Thinking about that is like thinking about lightning striking me dead. It never occurs to me. Yet the event I never thought of actually happened, but still God was in control and I am fine.

In the Old Testament portion of the Bible, a guy named Job has everything go wrong. Everything. A bunch of heavy things are happening in this story as God and Satan are having a major interaction. Yet in the midst of his pain, one of the things he says is "What I feared has come upon me; what I dreaded has happened to me."[3] This tells me that while the things I fear aren't likely to happen, a seemingly sadistic

3. Job 3:25.

spiritual law says that the more I fixate on them, the more I invite them into my life.

God says, "The wicked man flees though no one pursues, but the righteous are as bold as a lion."[4] In other words, when you have illusions of things that aren't actually happening, it is a statement of how far you are from God. Those who are not fearful and exhibit the boldness of a lion are those who have God and the ensuing marks of freedom.

I could put caveats around these statements and this whole book. But I'm not going to do that. I'm not going to let you off the hook. The reality of fear and the effects of strongholds are alive and well in your life. But you can do something about it. You can confront your strongholds and kick those bastards to the curb. You can push through the Blues and experience the Blessings on the other side. You can go through life with whole-hearted devotion to the ultimate Freedom Giver, and then the whole world wins with you first in line.

Where the Spirit of the Lord is, there is freedom.

A couple days ago I heard the "Battle Hymn of the Republic"—a song from the Civil War—and it was like hearing it again for the first time. Tucked away in the fifth verse is the line "As He died to make men holy, let us live to make men free." Chills went down my spine, and I thought, *Yes, I will live to make men free.*

This is what we're all invited to do: experience the real freedom God offers, and live to make others free.

Now go. Enjoy your freedom.

4. Proverbs 28:1.

WELCOME TO YOUR FREEDOM STORY.

Free Guide*

A companion guide to Brian Tome's *Free Book*

*As in freedom. (Not $0.00.)

THOMAS NELSON, INC.
Since 1798

Congratulations. You just accomplished your first dive into the waters of freedom.

Hopefully you are already feeling the positive effects. But freedom is a journey. Unfortunately, it's normally a longer journey than we would like. You probably still have some hang-ups in your day-to-day life that keep you from living and feeling fully free. If you are ready to take new land, then the *Free Guide** is designed to get you there. It isn't your typical workbook. It's an interactive guide to discovering what's holding you back from the free, full life God intends for you. *Free Guide* walks you through four of the most common strongholds and provides an action plan that will serve you in breaking free and enjoying life.

* *Where the Spirit of the Lord is, there is freedom.*

www.ThomasNelson.com

FELT THE PULL OF GOD?
ANSWERED IT?
FREAKED OUT ABOUT WHAT TO DO NEXT?

"The Revolution," as Tome calls the Christian life, is already underway, and while it is both exhilarating and fulfilling, it's challenging and confusing at times. This book will guide the reader from the basics (navigating through Christian kitsch at the bookstore) to the practical (Bible reading and building community) to the profound (concepts of forgiveness and using imagination in prayer). To those people who have previously dismissed the "Christian" life, or those who want to learn more about God in an accessible way, this book will be the breath that clears the air and shows them how to follow a Revolutionary God.

As Brian Tome was talking to a new Christ-follower in his office, he realized that he had nothing on his bookshelf that would give her the "straight talk" on the radical new life she was about to begin. So he wrote *Welcome to the Revolution*, a bold, honest, humorous guide to joining the ever-advancing Kingdom of God.

 THOMAS NELSON, INC.
Since 1798
www.ThomasNelson.com